FRONTIER KANSAS JAILS

FRONTIER KANSAS JAILS

GERALD J. BAYENS

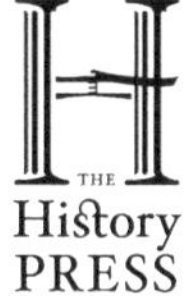

Published by The History Press
Charleston, SC
www.historypress.net

Images are courtesy of the author unless otherwise noted.

First published 2017

Manufactured in the United States

ISBN 978.1.46713.776.8

Library of Congress Control Number: 2016950702

Notice: The information in this book is true and complete to the best of our knowledge. It is offered without guarantee on the part of the author or The History Press. The author and The History Press disclaim all liability in connection with the use of this book.

CONTENTS

CONTENTS

ACKNOWLEDGEMENTS

A great deal of gratitude is owed to many people who encouraged and helped me in the process of writing this book. First and foremost, I would like to thank Washburn University for extending both an academic sabbatical and major research grant award, without which it would not have been possible to undertake such an exciting and fulfilling project.

I would also like to thank everyone who took the time to read the manuscript and make suggestions that I know made the book a better read. I am blessed to have so many terrific friends and supporters. While acknowledging every reviewer would undoubtedly result in an incomplete list, I do want to especially recognize Scott Heidner. A native of Berryton, Kansas, and a lifelong Kansas history enthusiast, Scott provided the initial structural and line editing of the book. He also provided a great deal of advice and encouragement throughout the writing of the book. In like fashion, many thanks to Ben Gibson, commissioning editor; Jaime Muehl, senior production editor; and the other good folks at The History Press for producing and marketing the book.

Lastly, a special thank-you goes to my wife, Joan Ann. She is my constant source of inspiration.

INTRODUCTION

Across the United States, there are three thousand city and county jails. Most are small in size, holding 49 or fewer prisoners, and are administered by a local criminal justice agency, such as a sheriff's office or local corrections department. Each year, 12 million people are admitted to jail after being arrested but not yet convicted of a crime. As a rule, most people who enter jail are released within a few hours or days. A smaller number of individuals are destined to become physically confined and deprived of their freedom. These prisoners are primarily adults who are awaiting trial on felony criminal charges. On any given day, nearly 800,000 people are incarcerated inside America's jails.[1]

In Kansas, ninety-eight jails are spread across the state, with the biggest facilities located in Wichita, Topeka and the Kansas City, Kansas metropolitan area. Jails across Kansas serve as the gatekeepers of the criminal justice system by sifting through the masses who enter its doors and keeping only those deemed necessary for lockup. In the early history of Kansas jails, this meant isolating bushwhackers, horse thieves and outlaws. Over time, the use of jail confinement expanded and became home to those who suffered from mental illness, those who had little money and those who had nowhere else to go. At present, more than six thousand people are locked up in Kansas jails every day. Some Kansas jails experience overcrowding conditions, and there are no formal state standards or provisions for jail inspection.

FRONTIER KANSAS JAILS

While the majority of citizens have a basic understanding about contemporary jails, they are likely to be less familiar with their beginnings. The story of the development of jails in Kansas is uniquely different from the history of jails in other states. The westward expansion of the frontier line into territorial Kansas during the mid-1800s entrusted law and order to the pioneers, and many did what they thought necessary to survive. When laws were written by proslavery officials, they were ignored by those who opposed slavery and believed Kansas should join the Union as a free state. Great violence erupted between the two rivals, and soon the newly settled territory would be recognized as "Bleeding Kansas." Political prisoners were confined in military encampments, private homes, storefronts and other makeshift jails. Leavenworth became the most populated territorial settlement and quickly known as "prison city." The first city jail in Kansas opened there in 1855.

As Leavenworth continued to grow and became the county seat, a courthouse and jail was built. In 1864, work began on the state's first penitentiary in Leavenworth County, near the site of what was known as the Oklahoma Jail—a portion of the Kansas State Penitentiary designated to house convicted felons from the Oklahoma Territory. A military prison was established in 1874 at Fort Leavenworth, later to become the United States Disciplinary Barracks. Lastly, in 1895, Congress authorized the construction of the federal prison system, and land was deeded to build the first United States Federal Penitentiary in Leavenworth. Construction of this penitentiary began two years later, with convict labor from inmates at Fort Leavenworth.[2]

A border war with Missouri ruffians occupied much of the history of Kansas shortly after statehood in 1861. When the jail population overflowed in Jackson County, Missouri, in 1863, the Union provost marshals decided that other buildings were to be used as jails in order to stifle problems caused by proslavery Missourians who opposed a free-state Kansas. One of those buildings was a three-story structure known as the Thomas Building, located in Kansas City. The second floor of this building was designated as a jail, even though large cracks appeared in the walls and ceilings and the timber beams were rotting. On the morning of August 13, 1863, the Thomas Building collapsed, and several young girls were killed, including the fourteen-year-old sister of Bill Anderson, known as "Bloody Bill," who rode with Confederate guerrilla William Quantrill. Many historians believe this event was viewed by Union soldiers as a deliberate act of murder and played an important role in Quantrill's decision to carry out the raid on Lawrence, Kansas.[3]

As the push into Kansas spread across the central and western parts of the state, local ordinances and statutes were legislated to cope with lawlessness. Great demands were placed on the sheriffs and city marshals to enforce the law and jail wrongdoers. Famous lawmen, such as Charlie Bassett, Wild Bill Hickok and Tom Smith, became legends based on their dealings with gunslingers, gamblers and outlaws in the cattle town jails of Abilene, Ellsworth and Dodge City. Vigilante groups formed in many communities, and the makeshift jails of earlier times were replaced by limestone, brick and concrete structures with iron cells and elaborate locking systems. Jails quickly became formal institutions across frontier Kansas during the late 1800s.

Why a Book on Kansas Jails?

While newspaper articles provide us with a glimpse into jails during the 1800s, no book has been written about frontier Kansas jails. The only essays directly associated with frontier jails were introduced by the American Prison Association in 1920, under the title *American Prison Association Semi-Centennial, 1870–1920: County Jails: In the Light of the Declaration of Principles of 1870*. This publication is a collection of articles written by prison reformers encouraging the American Prison Society to turn its attention to the county jails system. The papers include a presentation by Dr. Frederick Wines at the National Conference of Charities and Corrections of 1911 titled "The Abolition of the County Jail," together with a report of the special Jail Committee of 1907 prepared by Dr. Charles Henderson. Henderson's description provides some indication of jail conditions forty years after Kansas statehood:

> *No jail in Kansas is reported as crowded. Is that because it is virtually a prohibition State? But the jails of Kansas are not models. Rural and village jails usually have space enough for health, but they are among the worst for vile familiarities of association. The ordinary standard for judging whether a jail is crowded or not is too bad for a stable or cow shed, much less for human beings. This common standard is that, so long as men can find room in bunk, hammock or on stone floor, with a newspaper for a mattress, the place is spacious enough.*[4]

Frontier Kansas jails were greatly influenced by tales of deeds carried out by the people of the times. One of the earliest books on the history of Kansas is William Cutler's *History of the State of Kansas*, published in 1883 by Alfred (A.T.) Andreas in Chicago, Illinois. This large and elaborate book of more than 1,600 pages chronicles the early years of the territorial period. Cutler's role was that of managing editor and chief author. By the same token, stories of lawmen and outlaws in Abilene, Dodge City and other cattle towns captured the imagination of the country and were central to understanding the frontier era. Between the spring of 1960 and autumn of 1962, eleven articles appeared in the *Kansas Historical Quarterly* under the title "Some Notes on Kansas Cowtown Peace Officers and Gunfighters." In 1963, the collection of writings was published in a book titled *Why the West was Wild: A Contemporary Look at the Antics of Some Highly Publicized Kansas Cowtown Personalities*.[5] While these collections of historic materials pertain to the history of Kansas in the early years, none relates to jails.

In addition to the above-mentioned publications, small bits of information about Kansas jails are maintained by numerous county historical societies. Many of the jail buildings and their records have been registered with the U.S. Department of the Interior, National Park Service, as historic places. These records provide a cursory description of jail design and construction habits. For example, records from the Nemaha County Historical Society tell us that the old county jail in Seneca, Kansas, was a two-story brick structure built in October 1879 at the cost of $9,965. It was designed by P.J. Pauly, an architect from St. Louis, Missouri, who prepared plans, specifications and details for the jail. The original jail is described in Andreas's *History of the State of Kansas* as follows:

> *It is a two-story brick structure with an L, the main building, 32 x 25 feet, containing six rooms conveniently arranged for the residence of the jailor. The L, 29 x 26 feet, contains three of J. Pauly's patent steel cells, each of sufficient size to accommodate four persons, while above the jailor's residence are two rooms used for the incarceration of female prisoners and those retained for minor offenses. In connection with the building is a large cistern and facilities for using the water to the best advantage in case of fire.*[6]

Focus of this Book

When addressing American jails of the 1800s, authors focus almost exclusively on jails in the eastern part of the United States. This book is about Kansas jails and was written to provide a historical account of jails that were built during the great frontier era of American history, between 1854 and 1890. This half century is considered the settlement period and includes the Kansas territorial era, early statehood, the Civil War period and post–Civil War times to the end of the nineteenth century. This latter period is when the population of Kansas increased by the greatest amount in its history. The development of the materials contained within involve archival research of existing historical documents (e.g., legal records, jail ledgers, newspaper articles, etc.) and information from historical sites, museums and criminal justice agencies throughout the state of Kansas. The book is generally guided by two interrelated themes: First, what type of jails were built between 1854 and 1890, and where were they located in Kansas? Second, what significant events occurred during the operations of these frontier jails? Illustrations are included that depict the significant aspects of the story.

Part I

THE EARLY HISTORY OF JAILS

1
GAOLS IN ENGLAND

For most of human history, jails have served principally as holding places where offenders could be detained awaiting trial or pending the carrying out of a sentence by the court. Our introduction to jail history begins with the development of the tithing system in England. The tithe, in its simplest form, was a payment of one-tenth of the produce harvested from the land. The concept of tithing persisted into the first Anglo-Saxon code of law of the late sixth century, as small groups of people organized their village governance based on groups of ten. Cooperation and collective responsibility among villagers eventually resulted in the formatting of hundreds, which were groups of ten tithing. During the next two centuries, groups of hundreds banded together to form a new, higher unit of government called the shire (county). The chief law enforcement in each shire was the reeve, who was appointed by the Crown. The "shire reeve," or sheriff, was the local government official who represented the king in all local matters. He served the Crown directly, and his job was, in part, dependent on the social order found in his shire and the revenues he sent to the king. He also had the power to investigate and arrest those who violated customary laws. Because offenders had to be kept secure until they could appear before the king's courts, the sheriff was charged with care and custody responsibilities. To meet this demand, the county gaol (original word for jail) came into existence.[7]

In 1166, King Henry II, through the Assizes of Clarendon (a document establishing the foundation for English common law), required the sheriff of each English county to establish a gaol. The early models were constructed of wood (called the "king's timber"), no more than sheds set up beneath the city walls or attached to a castle.[8] Some of the gaols were located in preexisting structures such as towers, cellars and dungeons. In some cases, they consisted of only a single room and, in others, multiple chambers. These structures were damp, cold and miserable. No attempt was made to segregate prisoners by sex, age or seriousness of crime. Men and women (often with their children) were all confined together. Sometimes the prisoners had to wait in gaol for months before they were taken to trial. The prisoners were completely dependent on their families and friends for survival. If they had the means, they were well clothed and fed, and if not, they might starve or die from exposure.

Overcrowding was also a critical problem in English gaols. Not only did overcrowding aggravate the conditions in which the prisoners lived, but it also severely taxed the resources of the gaol, particularly the food supply. Though inmates were required to pay for their food, local famines, poor harvests and the presence of thieves, who regularly stole food en route to the prisoners, severely strained the gaol's food supply. As a result of both food shortage and overcrowding, many prisoners died in the gaol before reaching their day in court.

Following the signing of the Magna Carta by King John of England in 1215, the Crown could no longer imprison or execute subjects unless they were first tried by a jury of fellow citizens. The Magna Carta not only guaranteed English citizens basic rights but also authorized use of the gaol as a form of punishment.[9] In 1333, Hexham Gaol was built in northern England and was reputed to be the earliest confinement facility in England that held persons accused of crimes. Until the 1800s, thousands of prisoners passed through its doors while waiting for their trials in the nearby Moothall courtroom. Medieval justice required courts to meet only every few months, so a prisoner's mental and physical well-being was challenged often. The gaol at Hexham was rectangular in design, fifty-four feet high by fifty-nine feet long and thirty-six feet wide. The outer walls were nearly eight feet thick, encasing three floors that separated prisoners. Where prisoners were placed inside these walls was largely based on their wealth. The first and ground floors held prisoners who could afford to pay for better food and conditions. The dungeon, with its twenty-foot drop, held the poorest, who relied on friends or the church for food. A newel stair connected the floors, and iron shackles were readily available for the gaoler's use. Maintaining order was John de Cawood, appointed gaoler at a salary of two pence a day.[10] In the time of medieval justice, inflicting pain and torture was an accepted form

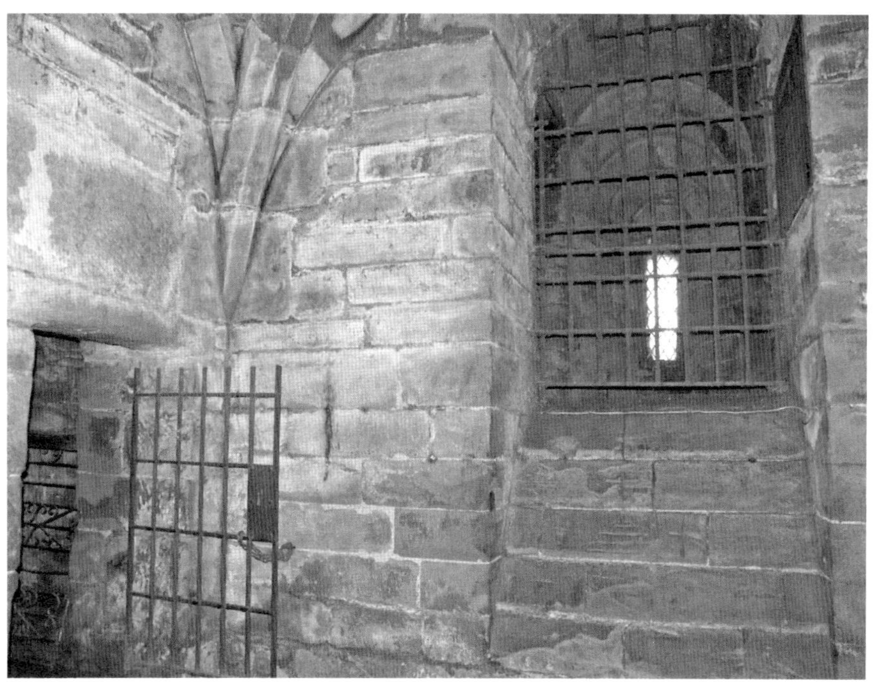

Prisoner cells in a castle dungeon. *Courtesy Kirk Bauer.*

of punishment. A gaoler was a powerful authority figure who could order prisoners to be placed in stocks and other restraint devices.[11]

Stocks had been set up in every gaol by the fourteenth century and were used mainly to restrain prisoners awaiting trial. Typically made of wood, the device partially immobilized a prisoner by locking his feet in place, sometimes with hands chained together. More elaborate variations included additional holes to confine the victim's hands. Ironically, this practice was originally developed as a means of publicly shaming offenders in hopes of deterring them from reoffending. Stocks had proved to be an effective labor-saving punishment, especially for persons guilty of minor infractions of the law, in lieu of sending them to gaol. In 1623, for example, stocks were officially designated as the punishment for drunkenness in England.[12]

Another apparatus commonly used to physically punish a prisoner was the pillory. This contraption was similar to stocks, with the added restraint of an individual's head and limbs. The wooden restraint was fixed to the top of a central post, forcing the occupant to stand. Pillories could also be used to restrain a victim while he or she was being whipped. Oftentimes,

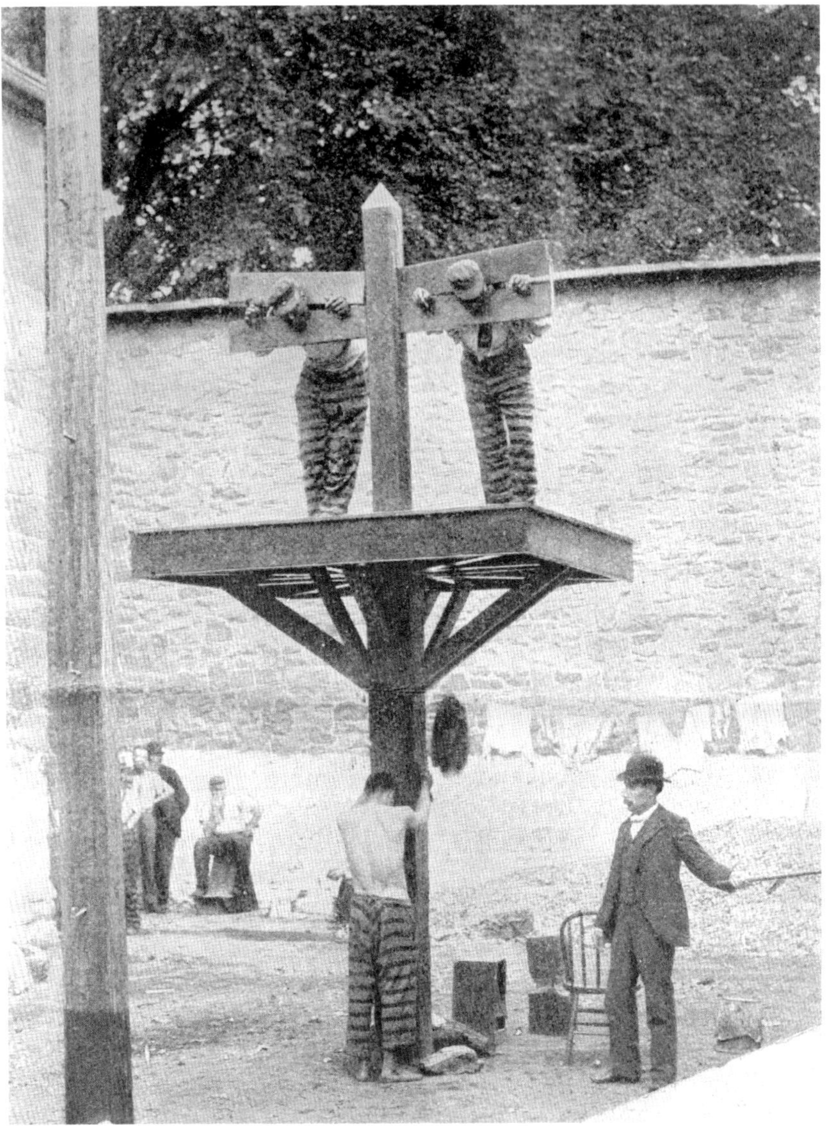

Two prisoners in a pillory, with another tied to a whipping post. *Library of Congress.*

the pillory was placed outside the gaol to increase public visibility of the punished offender.

English gaols remained pretty much the same well into the seventeenth century. They were terrible places in which to be confined and unpleasant to visit. In the words of prison reformer John Howard:

> *The prisoners were kept in close rooms, cells, and clammy dungeons 14 or 15 hours out of the 24. The floors of some of those caverns were very damp—in some of them there was an inch or two of water, and straw, or miserable bedding, was laid on the floors. There were seldom any bedsteads in them, and the air was offensive beyond expression.*[13]

Lack of cleanliness and proper ventilation resulted in the prevalence of typhus fever, known also by the name of gaol fever. Howard noted that, "from my own observations…I was fully convinced that more prisoners were destroyed by it [fever] than were put to death by all the public executions in the kingdom."[14]

Goals did get bigger during this time and were capable of holding more people. Although they were known as the "king's gaols," they were generally built by the counties and municipalities at their own expense. But once built, the local authority bore no financial responsibility for upkeep of their operation and maintenance. The prisoners were still charged with supporting themselves. Serious offenders were often transported to banishment or exile. Banishment also provided a means for England to rid itself of its nuisances and the unwanted and to partially relieve overcrowding.

2

BANISHMENT

In the early eighteenth century, the British Parliament enacted the Piracy Act, establishing a seven-year forced deportation to North America as punishment for those convicted of less serious felonies or as a possible sentence to which capital punishment might be commuted by royal pardon. In effect, this act formally designated America as England's penal colony. An estimated fifty thousand criminals were transported to America. England not only transported convicted felons to America but also transmitted its practices regarding other forms of punishment and criminal law in general. The practices of flogging—holding persons in stocks or pillories while subjecting them to ridicule—and branding were found in the American colonies. In Virginia, a law required that

> *the court in every country shall cause to be set up near the courthouse, a pillory, a pair of stocks, a whipping post, and a ducking stool, in such places as they shall think convenient, which not being set up in six months after the date of this act, the said Court shall be fined 5,000 pounds of tobacco.*[15]

The practice of banishment to the colonies ceased at the beginning of the American Revolution, as many of these new Americans took up arms against their native Britain. While an alternative destination was being considered, calls for new prisons to be built, coupled with efforts that emphasized inmate labor, led to the use of prison hulks, which were floating gaols on decommissioned naval vessels and old merchant ships. Anchored along the banks at various ports such as Portsmouth and Plymouth, these hulks imprisoned convicts who labored on the docks or dredging the river. At night, prisoners were chained to their bunks to prevent them from escaping to shore. The appalling conditions on the hulks, especially the lack of control and poor physical conditions, eventually led to the end of this practice. But the use of prison hulks did much to persuade public opinion that incarceration, with hard labor, was a viable penalty for crime.[16] Ultimately, convicted offenders were sent to Australia, a practice that continued between 1788 and 1850.[17] The merchant ship *Success* is arguably the most famous example of a convict ship used in the 1850s to transport British convicts to Australia. Life on this floating gaol meant the possibility of being subjected to severe discipline:

> *The "Success" in the days of her activity carried 80 pairs of handcuffs and 300 basils with chains for use on the voyage. Convicts made the voyage in irons all the way. It saved trouble. Charges of attempted or intended mutiny were trumped up. Governor Hunter mentions a case where "in consequence of some conjecture that they meant to seize the ship and murder the officers," the whole human cargo was double-ironed for the entire voyage. "They look most wretched from their long confinement," he added with simple neatness. On another occasion intended mutiny was disclosed to the captain by a convict. The captain could only induce the soldiers and sailors to spare lives by tempting them with the offer of a wholesale flogging in which each should take his part. "At eleven o'clock we commenced flogging these villains at the gangway, continued engaged at that service until 42 men and 8 women received their punishment."*[18]

It is estimated that 150,000 convicts were banished to Norfolk Island, Tasmania, and nine other penal colonies in Australia.[19] Captain Arthur Phillip (1738–1814), a career naval officer, was charged with setting up the first penal colony in Australia. On January 26, 1788, 1,030 persons went ashore at Port Jackson (later Sydney) in southeastern Australia. More than 700 were offenders, convicted of various crimes against the British Crown, including 188 women with their children, along with 252 naval seamen, marine guards and civilians with their families. As the first governor of Australia, Phillip was seen as a caring humanitarian who possessed a great sense of moral responsibility for others. He rejected a movement toward allowing slavery in the new colony and maintained that punishment of convicts should be based

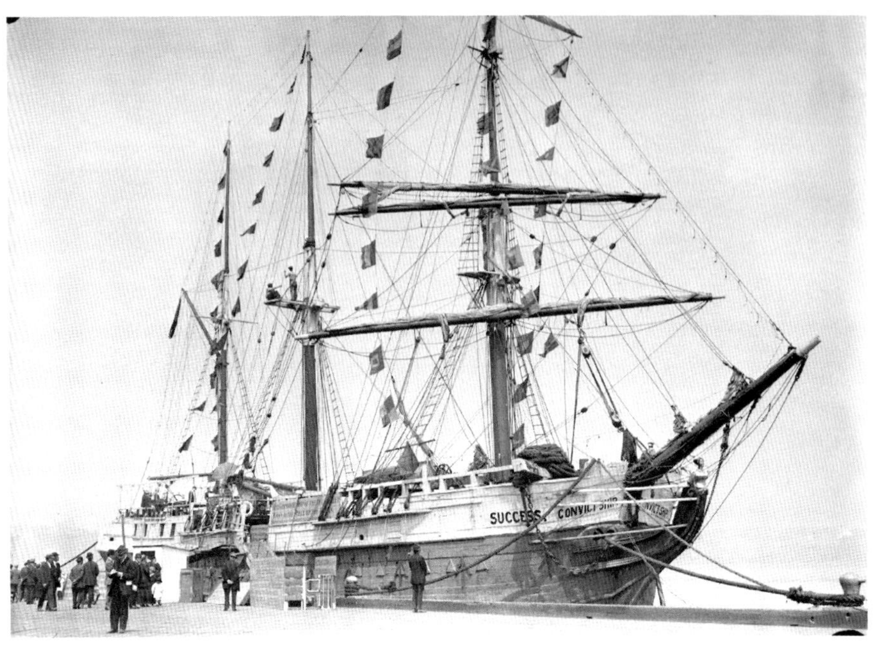

Convict ship *Success*, 1840. *Library of Congress.*

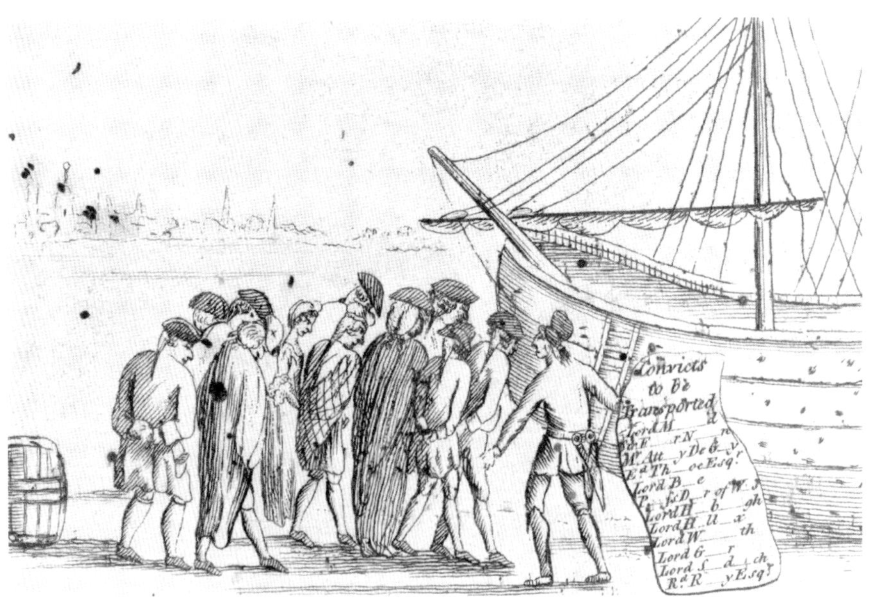

Drawing of political prisoners being boarded onto a convict ship. *Library of Congress.*

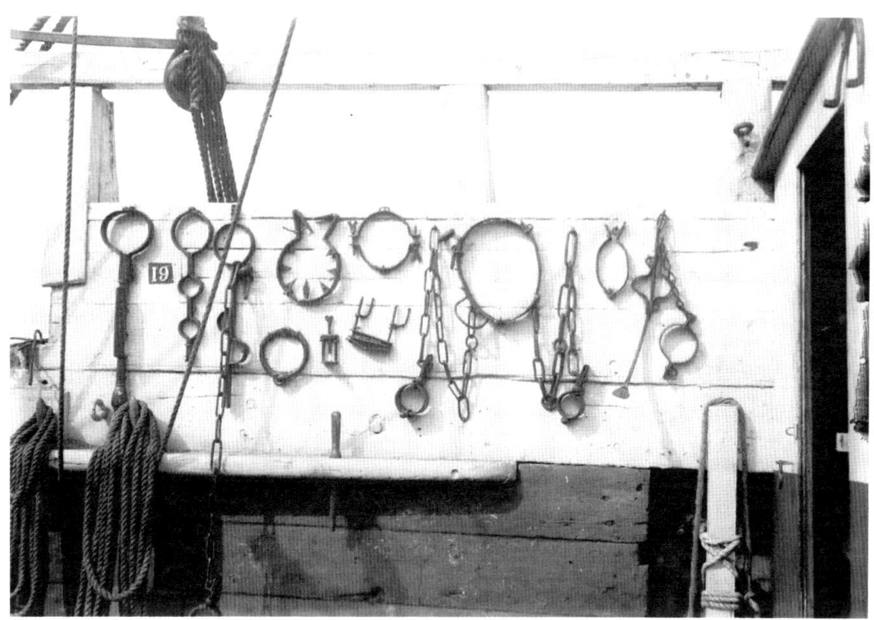

Torture irons on the convict ship *Success*. *Library of Congress.*

more on the principle of rehabilitation. Phillip founded a labor scheme in which people, whatever their crime, were employed according to their skills (e.g., brick makers, carpenters, nurses, servants).[20]

3

THE FIRST AMERICAN JAILS

Jails similar to those found in England were constructed in colonial America shortly after the arrival of the Pilgrims in 1620. One such jail is found in Barnstable, Massachusetts. Its historical prominence as one of the original towns of 1639 and its geographical position led to its selection as the shire town when the county was organized in 1685. It was constructed about 1690 and is touted as being the oldest wooden jail in America.[21] The building was constructed of solid oak beams with double planks nailed together every few inches with six-inch spikes. A court directive written in 1757 ordered the building of a new jail, but it was never erected. The old jail was used until 1820, when a new stone jail was built in the center of town. A description of the sort of prisoner held in Barnstable Jail is provided by the Prison Discipline Society in Boston:

> *Three men in room No. 1; all concerned in the riot at Provincetown, in which Thomas Rogers was murdered. All were in liquor at the time the murder was committed. Four young men, in room No. 3; all concerned in the same murder. One of the young men, in this room, said he was in company with Rogers when he was killed, and he was knocked down himself in the riot. They had been to the store together, he said, and had been drinking. These seven young men, three of them twenty-one, and three of them nineteen, and one of them eighteen years of age, and three of them educated in the public schools in Boston, are all in jail for murder, where they must remain several months before trial; all in consequence of the one*

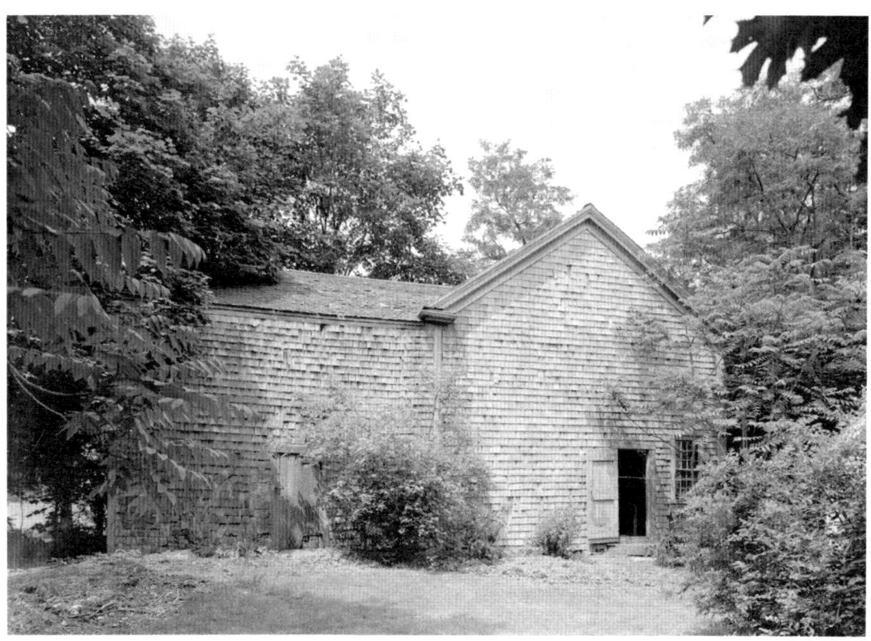

View of the south side of the 1690 Barnstable County, Massachusetts gaol. *Library of Congress.*

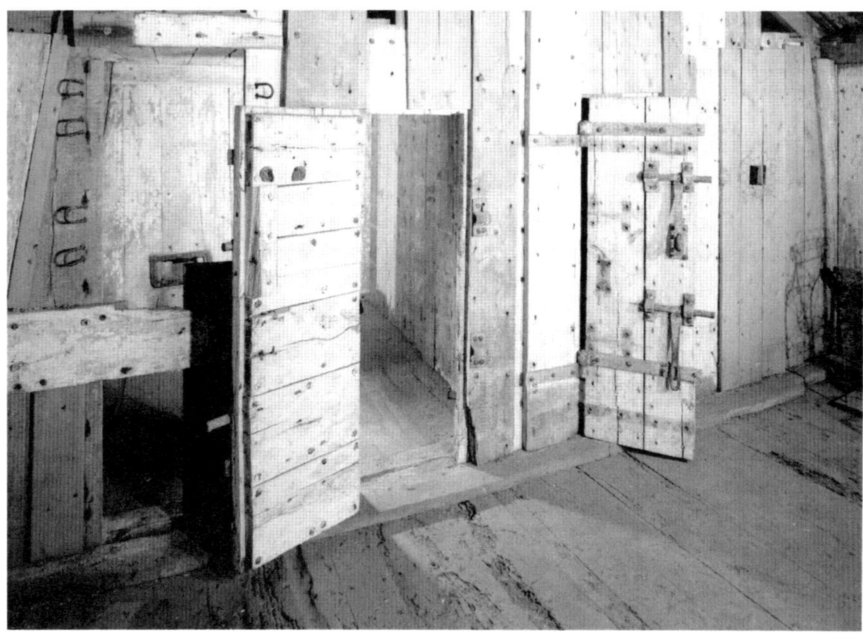

Entrance to the second-floor jail cells at the Barnstable County, Massachusetts gaol. *Library of Congress.*

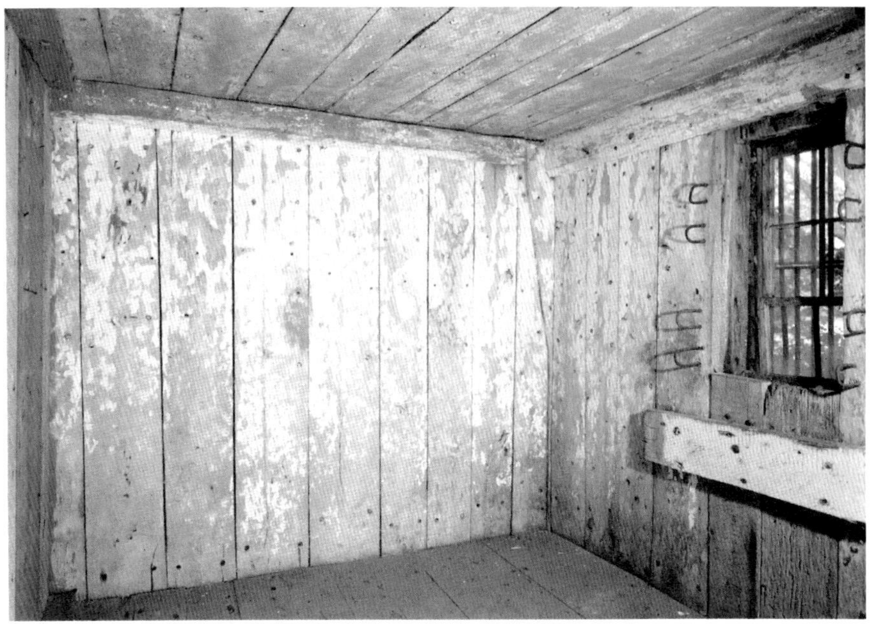

Jail cell on the north side of the second floor of the Barnstable County, Massachusetts gaol. *Library of Congress.*

> *drunken frolic. Three other men in this Jail—character unknown, in regard to temperance.*[22]

Like their English predecessors, early American jails housed defendants awaiting trial or convicted offenders awaiting the imposition of their sentences. The idea of serving a sentence in a confinement facility was reserved to Newgate Prison, which was intended for long-term punishment rather than pretrial detention. Newgate Prison, located in Simsbury, Connecticut, was actually an abandoned copper mine, with a guardhouse (commonly referred to as the stone jug) constructed over the mine's shaft.[23] Many of its prisoners were Tories who supported the British cause in the American Revolution. They were confined underground, in the dripping water and foul air of the long mine shafts, in what was essentially a dungeon. The daily routine at the prison was anything but pleasant:

> *The hatches were opened and the prisoners called out of their dungeon each morning at daylight, and three were ordered to "heave" up at a time; a guard followed the three to their shops, placing them at their work, and chaining those to the block whose tempers were thought to require it. All were brought*

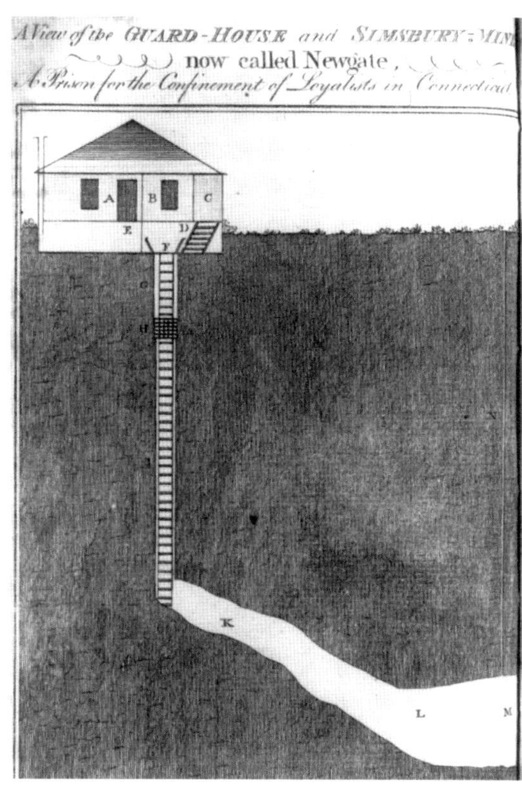

View of the guardhouse and Simsbury mines. *Library of Congress.*

out likewise in squads of three, and each followed by a guard. To those who never saw the operation, their appearance cannot be truly conceived, as they vaulted forth from the dungeon in their blackness, their chains clanking at every step, and their eyes flashing fire upon the bystanders around. It resembled, perhaps more than anything, the belching from the bottomless pit. After a while their rations for the day were carried to them in their several shops. They consisted for one day of one pound of beef or three-fourths of a pound of pork, one pound of bread, one bushel of potatoes for each fifty rations, and one pint of cider to every man. Each one divided his own rations for the day to suit himself—some cooked over their own mess in a small kettle at their leisure, while others, disregarding ceremonies, seized their allowance and ate it on an anvil or block. The scene was really graphic, and might remind one of a motley company of foreign emigrants on the deck of a canal-boat, during their journey to the "far West." They were allowed to swap rations, exchange commodities, barter, buy and sell, at their pleasure. Some would swap their rations for cider, and often would get so tipsy they could not work, and would "reel to and fro like a drunken man."[24]

As one might predict, Newgate Prison was the scene of several riots and escape attempts. The most successful escape occurred in May 1781, when a prisoner's wife insisted that she be incarcerated alongside her husband. When two guards started to admit her into the cavern by raising the passage hatch, several prisoners rushed them and seized the fixed-bayonet muskets of the other guards, who were asleep at the time. A violent attack ensued, leaving one guard dead and six others seriously wounded. The prisoners forced the guards into the dungeon and made their escape.[25]

In stark contrast to Newgate, the first institution designed for reform and considered by most historians to be the first "modern" American jail was the Walnut Street Jail in Philadelphia. It was built in February 1773 to replace the High Street Jail, which was constructed shortly after the English laws of 1718 went into effect. The High Street Jail consisted of two buildings: one for criminals, and the other for debtors, runaway apprentices and the idle poor. The new Walnut Street facility was to stress hard labor and be both "workhouse and house of correction in the City of Philadelphia."[26] The jail began to receive prisoners in January 1776, and some 105 prisoners were moved to their new quarters from the old High Street facility. The building was constructed of rough-hewn stone and designed to appear harsh. The main entrance led to a passageway through two iron-grated doors. Once they entered, prisoners were placed in one of eight arched rooms. The jail housed primarily pretrial detainees and prisoners awaiting imposition of their sentences. Conditions at the jail were appalling, with men and women, adults and children, thieves and murderers all confined together. Jailors made little effort to protect the prisoners from one another. Instead, they sold the prisoners alcohol and food, and clothing often came at a price. In the period when this facility functioned as a jail under local control, an inspection committee provided the following description of the Walnut Street Jail and its problems:

> *It is represented as a scene of promiscuous and unrestricted intercourse, and universal riot and debauchery. There was no labor, no separation of those accused, but yet untried, nor even of those confined for debt only from convicts sentenced for the foulest crimes, no separation by color, age or sex, by day or by night. The prisoners lie promiscuously on the floor, most of them without anything like bed or bedding.... Intoxicating liquors abounded and indeed were freely sold as a bar kept by one of the officers of the prison...*
>
> *Prisoners tried and acquitted were still detained till they should pay jail fees to the keeper and the custom of garnish was established and questioned, that is, the custom of stripping every newcomer of his own clothing to be sold for liquor, unless redeemed by payment of sum of money.*[27]

There were escapes at the Walnut Street Jail. For instance, in the spring of 1789, twenty-two prisoners seized and robbed the jailer and then threw him into the dungeon. Six of the twenty-two managed to escape before other jailers discovered the plot. As a result of these types of incidents, a block of cells was built in the courtyard for hardened offenders in 1790. This was known as the "Penitentiary House," the first use of this name on record. This was a brick building, three stories high, that contained sixteen solitary confinement cells. Prisoners slept on mattresses in their cells and received one meal a day, typically a small amount of pudding mixed with molasses. During their entire confinement, prisoners were not allowed to walk outside their cell.[28]

As a result of these conditions, the Quakers began to advocate and effect changes in jails. In Philadelphia, a group of citizens organized the Philadelphia Society for Alleviating the Miseries of Public Persons (a name it retained for one hundred years, at which time it became the Pennsylvania Prison Society).[29] Led by prominent citizens such as Benjamin Franklin and Benjamin Rush, the group became one of the most influential organizations for criminal confinement reform. Reform after the American Revolution was aimed not only at the institution but also at the criminal code. The Quakers contended that the sole end of punishment was the prevention of crime. They believed that the punishment should fit the crime and that confinement should involve penitence in which offenders could reflect on their crimes and emerge as better men and women.

Due to legislation in Pennsylvania from 1789 to 1794, the Walnut Street Jail was converted from a jail to a prison and provided for the solitary employment of inmates in prison workshops. Ultimately, the concept of solitary confinement and repentance was incorporated in the construction of the Eastern State Penitentiary at Philadelphia in 1829. In 1834, William Crawford visited the penitentiary and described its appearance as follows:

> *The penitentiary is situated about a mile from the city of Philadelphia. The site occupies about twelve acres. It is built of stone and surrounded by a wall thirty feet in height. Every room is vaulted and fireproof. At each angle of the boundary wall is a tower for the purpose of overlooking the establishment. In the centre is a circular building, or observatory, from which several corridors radiate: they are under complete inspection. The cells are ranged on each side of the corridors in the wall of which is a small aperture and iron door to each cell: through this aperture the meals of the prisoner are handed to him without his seeing the officer, and he may at all times be thus inspected without his knowledge…*[30]

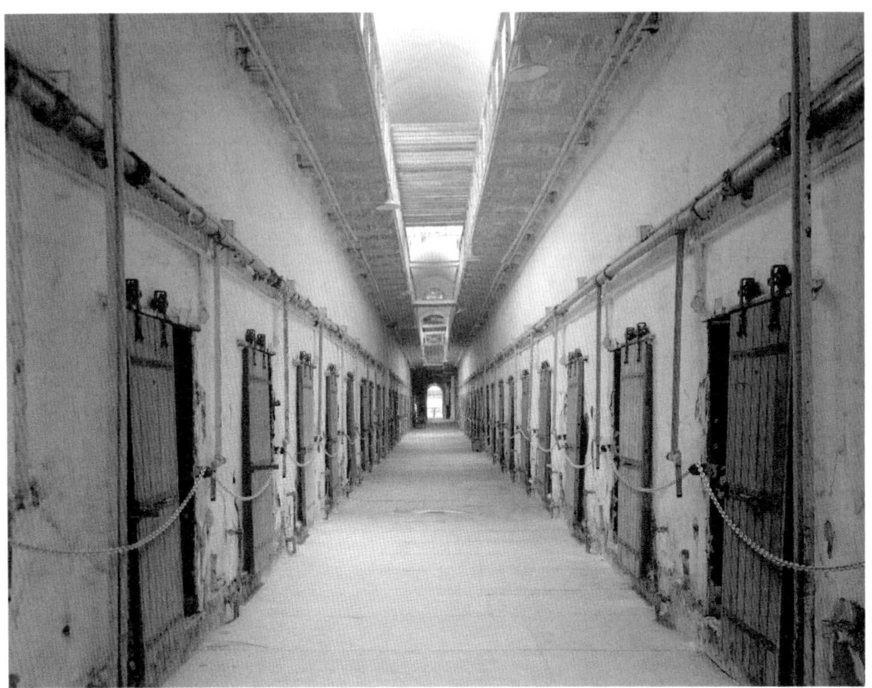

Eastern State Penitentiary cellblock in Philadelphia, Pennsylvania. *Library of Congress.*

The system of complete isolation from other prisoners came to be known as the Pennsylvania system and was copied in both America and Europe. Soon, a dispute regarding the most appropriate form of prison programs and architecture developed in America. In the early 1800s, advocates of the Pennsylvania system were challenged by supporters of the Auburn (New York) system, a method of imprisonment that utilized solitary confinement in small cells during the evening but provided congregate labor during the day to maximize the profit obtained from inmate labor. Solitary confinement, therefore, was not commonplace except for those notable criminals who would have been condemned to death. By 1820, the Walnut Street Jail experienced so much overcrowding that it reverted back to a jail. When a new county prison opened in 1835, Walnut Street's institutional life came to an end.[31]

By the mid-1850s, both local jails and state prisons had been firmly established in America. The Auburn system had prevailed, in large measure because of its economy of operation, and cities began to build large county and city jails. Although these new jails were built to remove, manage, punish and reform problem populations, their development was based on no clear plan. They were merely "super secure, fenced, ugly, uncomfortable and unsafe, totally deprived environments."[32] Jails in many places housed those awaiting trial and serving sentences and, in some locations, those being held as witnesses. Scattered among this population were children, debtors, slaves and both the mentally and physically ill. Debtors who had played such a prominent role in the jail population eventually began to disappear from it. Debt in colonial America had been an offense for which one could be imprisoned. Later, it became more difficult to jail an individual for this offense alone, and imprisonment for debt was generally abolished.

Although children had always been housed in jails, trends developed in which youths were separated from the adult male inmates. In some facilities, juveniles were placed with female inmates, while in other places they were segregated and placed adjacent to the women's wards. Increasingly, they were kept in a completely separate section of the jail because the county or city lacked separate juvenile facilities. They were temporarily transferred to jail if they had severe behavior problems and were likely to stay there until their hearings or the disposition of their cases. As the years passed, progressively fewer juveniles were confined in jail.

Jail and prison reform continued into the early nineteenth century, and many of the progressive changes were due to the efforts of reform groups. One of the best-known reform groups of the times was the Boston Prison Discipline Society. This group, founded by theology student Theodore Dwight, was concerned with "every class subjected to confinement in prison, the criminal, debtor and the insane."[33] The society's reports, issued from 1829 to 1855, suggest that the Auburn design was favored as the approach to incarceration for jails of the period. This proved to be significant because nearly all other reform efforts in penology during the nineteenth and first half of the twentieth centuries dealt with conditions of custodial prisons and alternatives to prison, such as reformatories, probation and parole. So the emphasis of reform was on prisons not on jails.

From 1780 to 1860, the typical American jail was a relatively small structure, frequently located in the seat of a rural county. These buildings were vastly different in condition, population, structure and management. There were those built for only one or two inmates and those that could house hundreds. Many eastern jails (e.g., Boston, New York and Philadelphia) generally held several hundred prisoners. Their Auburn style of architecture dictated that jails were built as massive concrete and metal constructions resembling fortresses on the outside and cages on the inside. The belief that prisoners must be constrained was overemphasized in the architecture and furnishings, as a need to control prisoners was evident in this jail design. In the typical large jail facility, inmates were housed in two-, four-, six- and eight-person cells or in multiple-occupancy dormitories. Jail cells consisted of at least one wall made of iron bars; the other three were cement, cinder block or steel. The bars gave the cell its cage-like appearance and allowed jail guards to view the prisoners.[34]

In the South, poorly constructed jails were frequently the standard. In 1854, citizens of Whitfield County, Georgia, built a wooden jail for $189.50. Five years later, the timbers of the jail were "almost entirely rotten, so much so that prisoners cannot be kept there with any degree of safety."[35] Some sheriffs were forced to adopt methods seen as inhumane in order to maintain security. In New Orleans, for example, offenders were housed with hogs and often chained up.[36] New jails were needed, and the architects who designed newer structures tried to create the most secure facilities possible. Jail plans often proposed that the building be forty feet by twenty-four feet, with the external wall built of brick, two feet thick.[37] Problems with the rapidly growing jail population played a large role in the design of these facilities, especially after multiple embarrassing incidents regarding overcrowded jails had been reported. Because of these issues, circuit judges were required to conduct or oversee examinations of jails at least once a year to make sure there were not any outstanding concerns that needed to be fixed.

Along with the costs necessary to construct and maintain courthouses and jail facilities, it was very expensive to imprison people. One governor of Mississippi demanded immediate trials and banned undetermined times of imprisonment due to the amount of money it cost to hold prisoners in jail.[38] Similar measures were taken that allowed all prisoners except the ones being held for felonies to walk out of the jail as long as the jury believed they would abide by the decisions made in county court.[39]

Reformers had suggested that one of the worst things a prisoner could do was sit in jail without engaging in any productive activity. A few jails tried to remedy this situation by putting their inmates to work. This generally included small cleaning jobs inside the facility and other manual labor chores. An alternative to work in the jail was to work outside the facility under supervision. The road or chain gang, as it came to be known, was an alternative to sitting out one's time in a jail cell. In a number of southern states, county chain gang systems were conceived in which prisoners under the county control were used to build and repair public roads.

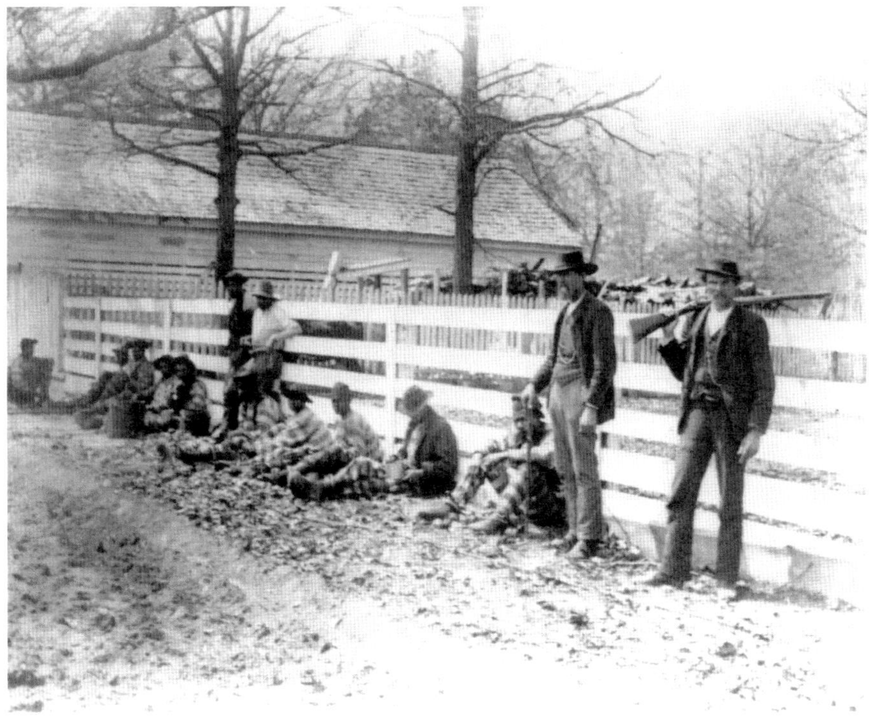

Chain gang prisoners and guards. *Library of Congress.*

Many of the southern states had no state prisons, so those convicted of crimes were sent to the county jails. Prisoners were sentenced to serve their time on road gangs, which meant being forced to dig ditches, construct roads or work in the fields. They were often chained together and housed in temporary camps adjacent to the work area. This provided the illusion of reducing the inmate population and consuming inmate idleness. But conditions in these camps were deplorable, often lacking proper bathing facilities. The food was poor, and shelter was minimal. A prisoner sentenced to five or more years on a road gang would likely not survive. Chain gangs eventually gave way to prisoner work crews that worked offsite and under guard, but not in chains. Portable jail wagons were sometimes used to transport prisoner work crews to the work site. Some were elaborate carriages holding iron bunks that unfolded from the walls. A heavy, waterproof canvas was dropped over the sides for warmth at night. These rolling cages were patented as "Jails for Sleeping Convicts," which mounted on wheels and had barred walls and rows of bunks arranged on opposite sides of a central aisle. They could be "easily moved from place to place by 6 mules."[40] Chain

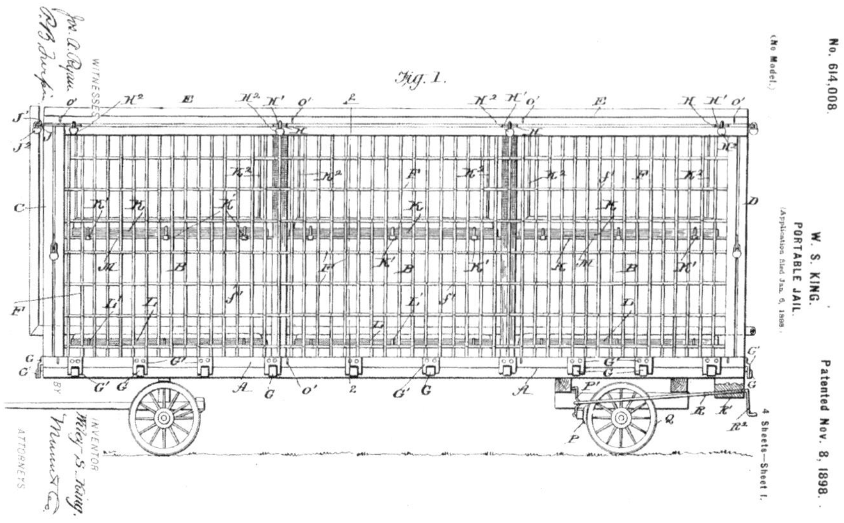

Schematic diagram of a portable jail wagon. *U.S. Patent and Trademark Office.*

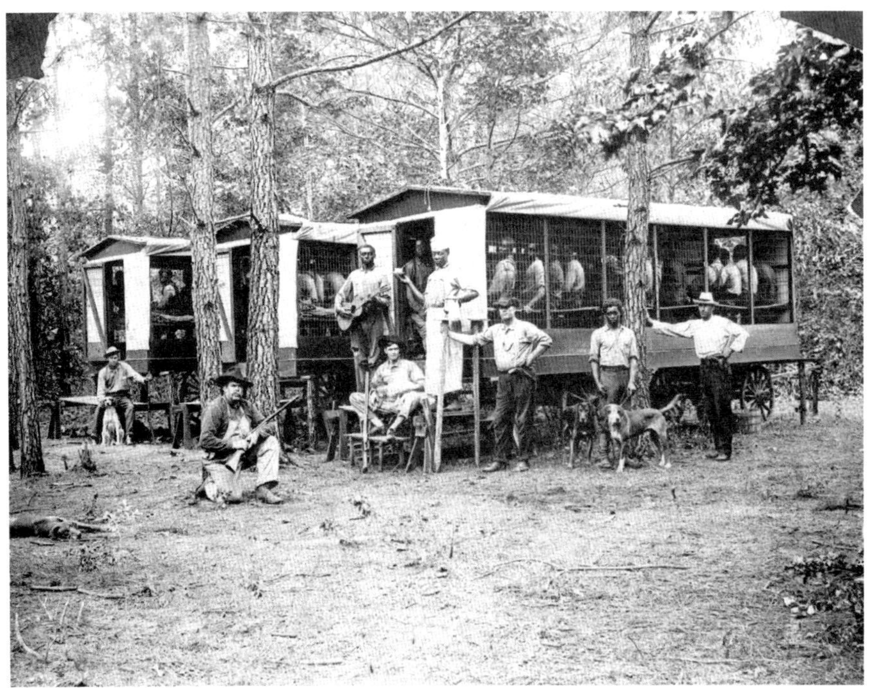

Chain gang road crew and their wagon quarters, which were equipped with bunks and moved from place to place as labor was needed. The dogs are bloodhounds used for running down any attempted escapees. *Library of Congress.*

gangs, work crews and other forms of forced convict labor would shape the historical development of local and state penal systems in the South.

By 1860, the United States had expanded far to the west of the Mississippi River. The discovery of gold in California brought thousands of settlers to the Pacific coast, and as a result of its exploding population and economy, it became a state. Most traveled the two-thousand-mile stretch of the Oregon Trail and settled in the Oregon Territory, including present-day Idaho; parts of Montana, Oregon and Washington; and western Wyoming. Jails built in these far-western regions of the United States were commonly referred to as calabooses. Calaboose comes from the Spanish word *calabozo*, meaning "dungeon." These jails were of simple design, typically holding a few people. They were administered by the sheriff or town marshal and functioned to confine individuals before trial. The jail also served as a holding facility for those convicted of serious offenses and waiting transportation to the territorial prison.

Between 1854 and 1890, several interrelated factors formed what we know about the history of Kansas jails in the frontier era. The first was the western expansion into the Kansas Territory through the Oregon, California and Santa Fe Trails. Along theses historic trails, military forts were established, and towns were incorporated that required the building of military stockade and city jails to detain those who broke the law. The availability of timber, limestone and other materials dictated how those jails would be built. Since hand labor was widespread, many of the first jails built in Kansas towns were inadequate to hold even the most unassuming prisoner. Consequently, escapes were frequent. Some of the more affluent towns purchased jail cells manufactured in Detroit, Chicago and St. Louis. The presence of prefabricated jails was commonplace as county seats were formed and courthouses built.

Another important historical factor was the establishment of cattle towns in frontier Kansas. Between the years of 1865 and 1885, hundreds of thousands of Texas Longhorns were driven to shipping points in Kansas towns such as Abilene, Ellsworth and Dodge City. Cowtowns quickly developed a reputation for violence and lawlessness, as hundreds of cowboys, gamblers and outlaws frequented saloons, brothels and gambling halls. Much of this activity gave birth to the reputations of famous lawmen such as Wild Bill Hickok, Wyatt Earp and Bat Masterson. Similarly, many of the notorious outlaws and fugitives began their careers by rustling cattle, stealing horses and robbing stagecoaches in Kansas. Cowtowns needed jails, and they were built.

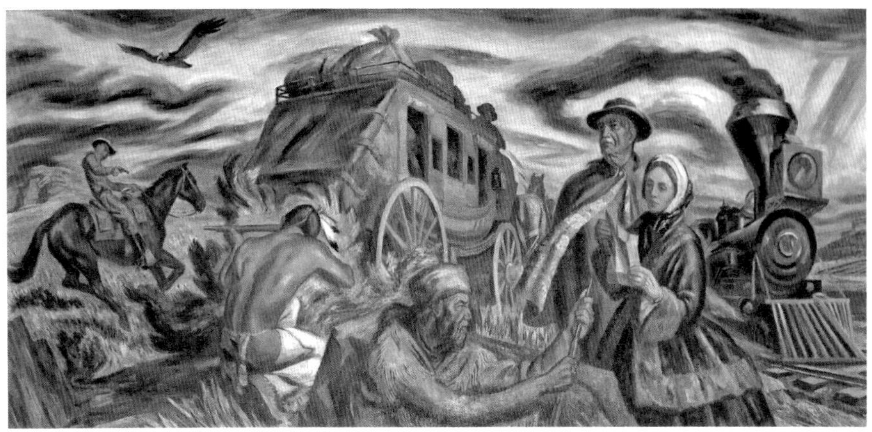

From 1854 to 1890, frontier Kansas emerged as a land where people of diverse backgrounds and varied intentions encountered and sometimes had conflicts with one another. *Library of Congress.*

Finally, the railroad expansion of the late 1800s played an important part in the history of Kansas jails. By the 1890s, more than 150,000 miles of track had been laid across America, making it possible for fast transportation into western lands. In Kansas, previously uninhabited lands soon became populated and organized into towns along the steel highway. Where towns had existed across the state, the railroad effectively changed modest settlements into urbanized communities, where hotels, opera houses, courthouses, jails and other modern buildings became commonplace. And of course, trains and the wealth they often carried became primary targets for bandits to rob.

In Kansas and throughout the country, jails were deplorable places. Most jails were unsanitary and impossible to keep clean. The inability to adequately heat these buildings resulted in keeping the windows shut much of the time. The disposal of sewage was difficult, leaving a rancid smell about the jail. To complicate problems, reform efforts concentrated on prisons, not jails.[41] So a general "out of sight, out of mind" attitude toward jails and their prisoners was established well before the migration into the Great Plains. Nevertheless, no matter how it was built or how badly it functioned, the jail in frontier America would be needed to lock up horse thieves, murderers, drunks and other lawbreakers—that is, if you weren't strung up by a lynch mob first.

Part II
THE NATION EXPANDS INTO TERRITORIAL KANSAS

Many people passed through the Kansas Territory, as the southern sections of the Kansas River were the starting points of the Oregon, California and Santa Fe Trails. An estimated 400,000 settlers went on these western migration trails between 1840 and 1860, and about 1 out of 10 died en route to the West.[42] The languages heard along the culturally diverse trails included English, Spanish, German, French, Dutch and those of several Native American Indian tribes. It's fitting to note that more than twenty tribes or remnants of tribes lived in the Kansas Territory. Many were migrants to the prairies, having been displaced by the 1830 Indian Removal Act, which caused 46,000 Native American Indians to leave the Great Lakes region, the Ohio Valley region and the South to relocate west of the Mississippi River.[43]

Two western Missouri border towns were significant to the western expansion into Kansas Territory and settlements along the trails. The first was St. Joseph, Missouri, which has been referred to as the "jumping-off point" for the thousands of America's pioneers as they traveled west along the Oregon Trail. It is estimated that as many as fifty thousand pioneers passed through St. Joseph in 1849 alone.[44] The town quickly developed into a rough frontier settlement, as covered wagons, oxen and supplies purchased by the migrants established the economic basis for the town. As feeder trails from the Oregon Trail were established across northeastern Kansas, towns such as Leavenworth, Lawrence and Lecompton sprang up along the Missouri and Kansas Rivers. These newly established Kansas settlements would be the primary sites of many battles between free-state and proslavery advocates that occurred between 1854 and 1865. Moreover, these towns played important roles in the development of jails and prisons on local, state and federal levels in Kansas.

The second border town of importance to the establishment of Kansas settlements was Westport Landing, which changed its name to the "City of Kansas" in 1853. It was an outfitting and starting point for traders, trappers and immigrants heading southwest on the Santa Fe Trail. The vast majority of the Santa Fe Trail ran through Kansas, much of it along the Arkansas River. After leaving Westport Landing, pioneers traveling on the Santa Fe Trail passed through Kansas townships such as Shawnee, Council Grove and Dodge City. A section of the trail was also used by immigrants on the California and Oregon Trails, branching off to the northwest near Gardner, Kansas. When a bridge was built in 1869, the population started to boom from only 4,400 at the 1860 census to 130,000 in 1889. The city changed its name from the City of Kansas to "Kansas City" in 1889 and annexed Westport in 1894.[45]

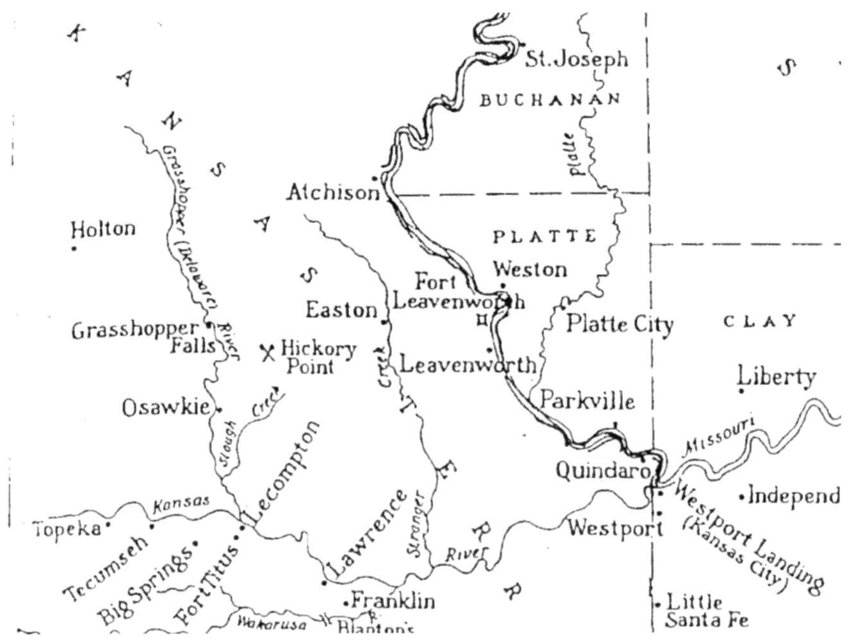

Map of Kansas-Missouri border towns in the mid-1800s.

By 1850, the resident population in America was a little over 23 million people within thirty-one states and four organized territories (Minnesota, New Mexico, Oregon and Utah). When the 1854 Kansas-Nebraska Act[46] created the territories of Kansas and Nebraska, only an estimated 800 squatters lived in the Kansas geographical area.[47] That same year, the Commonwealth of Massachusetts authorized the creation of the Massachusetts Emigrant Aid Company for the purpose of assisting and encouraging immigrants to settle in the West. Other smaller organizations, such as the Union Emigrant Aid Society and the Worchester County Massachusetts Aid Society, also rendered aid to migrants making the trip to the new territory of Kansas.[48] By February 1855, a census count (taken from voter lists) showed 2,905 residents in the Kansas Territory, with settlement patterns generally located in the eastern part of Kansas, along the transportation routes to the west.[49]

Many of these residents were anything but law abiding, and the Kansas Territory quickly earned a reputation for lawlessness. At the top of the list of outlaws were horse thieves, murderers and bushwhackers, the latter a name often used to describe predatory outlaws who prowled the land and struck their victims without warning. The origin of "bushwhacker" dates to the 1840s, when Washington Irving (author of *Rip Van Winkle* and *The Legend of Sleepy Hollow*) referred to "gallant bushwhackers" as woodsmen who knew how to fend for themselves in harsh environments. The name bushwhacker was also affixed to quasi-military forces that engaged in guerrilla warfare tactics prior to and during the Civil War era.[50] In the town of Nevada, Missouri, the conflict over states' rights and slavery led to so much bloodshed that, in 1863, the Federal militia burned the town to the ground, except for one building: the historic "Bushwhacker Jail." Constructed of native sandstone in 1860, prisoners were housed in cell blocks. Quarters for the sheriff and his family were added to the building in 1871. In October 1929, a grand jury called the jail "an insult to civilization and a disgrace to the county," yet it continued to be used for another thirty-one years.[51]

If these bushwhackers and other outlaws were captured, they quickly met their fate at the end of a rope, usually by "lynch law," a term that included every sort of punishment, including hanging, which might be inflicted by persons independent of legal authority. Such was the case in April 1858 in the frontier town of LeRoy, Kansas:

> *Just south of the old Indian cemetery at Burlington lived a family by the name of Claywell. Different members had been repeatedly arrested but there being no jails, they always managed to escape. Horse stealing was the particular offense of the two grown sons, and the citizens decided that the next time any of them committed a crime they would take things into their own hands. A short time after this conclusion had been reached one of the young men stole a horse from Le Roy and was arrested. Word was sent out and the citizens formed a court, with judge, jury, attorney for the defendant and attorney for the state. He was found guilty and, on vote of the mass who attended the trial, was hanged at Le Roy in presence of a vast throng of witnesses.*[52]

There were, of course, other types of crimes committed in the Kansas Territory besides horse stealing and murder. Some were just as serious (e.g., robbery, rape), echoing a similar general disrespect for basic human rights. Other less serious types of crime, such as larceny, tended to be crimes of opportunity. Yet most crimes committed were against civil order, such as public intoxication and disorderly conduct. As John Ingalls, U.S. senator for Kansas (1873–91), notes:

> *The curse and bane of frontier life is drunkenness. The literature of the mini-camp, the cross-roads, and the cattle ranch reeks with whiskey. In every new settlement the saloon precedes the schoolhouse and the church, is the rendezvous of ruffians, the harbor of criminals, the recruiting station of the murderer, the gambler, the harlot, and the thief…*[53]

Townships in the territory passed ordinances to protect property and forbid nuisance behaviors that ran contrary to civil order, including carrying a firearm in town. To deal with more serious offenses, judicial power was vested in a Supreme Court consisting of a chief justice and two associate justices.[54] There was also an appointed territorial attorney and a U.S. marshal. The temporary seat of government was located at Fort Leavenworth, and it was ordered that public buildings not in use for military purposes be occupied by the territorial officers. However, if ordinances and territorial laws were to be successful, the government needed regulators to enforce the law and jails to hold persons who broke the law.

First Judicial Officers of the Kansas Territory[55]

Official	Term(s)	Annual Salary
Governor Andrew Reeder	1854–1855	$2,500.00
Chief Justice Samuel Lecompte	1854–1859	$2,000.00
Associate Justice Saunders Johnston	1854–1855	$2,000.00
Associate Justice Rush Elmore	1854–1855; 1858–1861	$2,000.00
U.S. Marshal Israel Donalson	1854–1861	$300.00
U.S. Attorney Andrew Isack	1854–1857	$250.00

Protecting travel on the major trails was a priority of the U.S. government during the western expansion. Military forts were established at Fort Leavenworth (1827), Fort Scott (1842) and Fort Riley (1853), with U.S. mounted regular forces, commonly referred to as dragoons, serving both peacekeeping missions and exploratory expeditions. The town of Leavenworth was founded in 1854 largely to support Fort Leavenworth and is considered the first official settlement in Kansas.[56] Many of the settlers in Leavenworth were Missourians, some of proslavery sentiment and others proposing free-state status. Consequently, troops from Fort Leavenworth were frequently called on to respond to disturbances in town and surrounding areas. The military would continue to be heavily involved in the border conflict of subsequent years that pitted Missouri proslavery groups, "border ruffians," against antislavery groups, "jayhawkers," in Kansas.[57]

In the town of Leavenworth, many buildings were erected during the early settlement of the city, including several hotels, flour mills and breweries.[58] The town became incorporated in the summer of 1855, and soon city ordinances were enacted to curb behaviors such as disturbing the peace, discharging firearms and drunkenness. Saloons were abundant in nearly every township throughout the Kansas Territory, and Leavenworth was no exception. Most saloons stayed opened all night, and drunken brawls were commonplace, typically taking place outside the building in dark streets and alleyways. Normally, a fine was levied, but with money being scarce, many townships passed city ordinances allowing prisoners to work off their fines. Vagrancy was yet another problem that required a city ordinance. In Lawrence, an 1863 ordinance defined a vagrant as any person "found to be loitering, wandering or loafing about dramshops, saloons, restaurants or any other place by day or night without any visible and lawful means of support."[59] The first offense came with a minimum one-dollar fine, the second offense a minimum five-dollar fine and the third offense a minimum twenty-five-dollar fine. Later that year, ordinance 115 clarified that the city marshal had the power to arrest anyone for violating a city ordinance.[60]

Although ordinances typically required the perpetrator to pay a fine, many did not have the money to do so. Consequently, it was off to jail for those who were in debt to the city or committed more serious crimes. In November of that year, the city purchased a building for a jail at the price of $600, and special policemen were hired. The jail quickly became one of the most essential buildings in town, and detention jail cells were nearly always full with combatants awaiting their punishment. Prisoners were assigned hard labor, most often required to hammer huge rocks into smaller rocks that would be used to pave the streets of the town. Some prisoners were required to work on the streets, under the direction of the city marshal, or helped in paving the levee and other steamboat wharves. Prisoners worked ten hours a day, six days a week, and for every day's work, they earned $1 toward the payment of the fine and costs in their case.[61]

In January 1856, voters gathered in Leavenworth City to cast their ballots on the constitution that was framed and adopted at a Free State Convention held in Topeka. As in the previous elections, proslavery men resorted to violence in an attempt to deter the free-state men from voting. Ultimately, the ballot box was destroyed, the house of an antislavery citizen burned to the ground, a proslavery man helped to escape from jail and the jail burned.[62] Incidents involving local vigilantes occurred in attempts to restore order, as one account describes how local mobs kept "Missouri roughs and disreputable characters…in check":

> *An occasion offered in July, 1857, when James Stephens was foully murdered and robbed of $108 near the river. His murderers, John C. Quarles and W.M. Bayes, were taken from the jail and lynched on an old elm tree near the sawmill, despite the protestations of Judge Lecompte and other law-abiding citizens. He was threatened with personal violence himself, as also was the United States Marshal, who got on a box before the mob of over a thousand people and attempted to pacify them. The City Marshal and police were hustled out of the way. The crowd battered down the door of the Jail with a stick of timber, dragged Quarles forth and hung him to a tree. The noose was not properly tightened and for a moment the man managed to grasp the rope with his hands, but a heavy-*

> *set, brutal ruffian caught him by the feet, threw his whole weight upon him and strangled his victim to death. When the mob returned for Bayes there was more protesting by authorities, and Mrs. Bayes, fought them off line and infuriated beast, as she was. Bayes, however, followed in the steps of Quarles, except that he allowed his hands to be tied behind him and was swung off into eternity in a less horrible manner. William Knighten, a weak-minded young man, and Bill Woods, a counterfeiter, and alleged accomplices in the murder, were taken to Delaware City, tried, and finally discharged. This lynching affair seemed to check the reckless spirit of crime, which heretofore pervaded the city, and thereafter Leavenworth was more free from lawlessness than most of the other towns.*[63]

As Leavenworth continued to grow and became the county seat, a courthouse and jail was planned. In 1858, John G. Haskell was appointed to design a building about one hundred feet by two hundred feet in three wings, to cost about $100,000. The middle wing, sized to be about sixty feet by one hundred feet, was to be built at once, with accommodations for a jail in the basement at a cost of about $35,000. However, it was not until 1873 that the structure was built. Haskell would also design and build the Douglas County Jail in Lawrence, Kansas. He went on to design many important buildings in the state, including courthouses, university buildings, government buildings, schools, churches, hospitals and opera houses.[64] In the interim, the county housed prisoners in the city jail and erected a two-story stone and brick building on the north line of the courthouse square and about midway from Third to Fourth Streets. The first floor was occupied as a county jail, and the second story was used as the probate judge's office and courtroom and the sheriff's office.

In the jail yard, on the west side of the building, the first legal hanging in Leavenworth took place on February 13, 1863, when Carl Horne (sometimes reported as Horn) was hanged for the murder of Philip Friend.[65] The events that led to a criminal case started in June 1861, when Horne, a thirty-five-year-old former U.S. soldier, became a boarder at the house of Philip Friend, along with Friend's wife, Catharine, and their five-year-old son. In August, Friend was reported missing after his whereabouts were unknown for nearly two weeks. His body was discovered under some hay on his farm, and it was obvious that he had been bludgeoned to death. A few days prior to the discovery of Friend's remains, Horne and Friend's wife traveled to Leavenworth, where they were married. The newlyweds then headed east to Elmwood, Kansas, some forty miles away, near St. Joseph, Missouri.

U.S. marshals arrested the couple and brought them back to Leavenworth. Horne would ultimately confess to having murdered Friend with a steel axe. During the trial in November, the judge made several misleading statements to the jury regarding the supposition of Horne's guilt based on the atrocious nature of the crime. Horne was quickly convicted and sentenced to be hanged in January 1862. But Horne's attorneys appealed the case, and it was heard by the Kansas Supreme Court. The appeal was based on arguments that the judge's statements to the jury violated common law of a defendant's presumption of innocence. The court agreed, set aside the guilty verdict and remanded the case for retrial. Horne was retried, convicted and hanged. Catharine Friend was found guilty of second-degree murder and sentenced to ten years in prison.[66]

4

THE PRISON CITY

In addition to the city and county jail, Leavenworth County became home to three prisons: Kansas State Penitentiary, U.S. Military Prison and U.S. Penitentiary Leavenworth. The town quickly earned the reputation of being a prison city, and imprisonment as a form of punishment rapidly developed as the primary penalty for most crimes in the state. Being locked up in these penal strongholds meant being subjected to a multitude of painful practices employed by their keepers. A particular physical punishment that proliferated in Kansas during this period was known as the "alkazan." The prisoner was placed facedown in a heavy coffin, with hands and feet tied behind the back and drawn up so that movement was virtually impossible. The coffin lid was closed, and the prisoner lay in the dark for hours. A variation of this punishment was practiced when the prisoner was placed in an upright position, again tied immovably, with his mouth plugged open by a wedge and teeth, face and ears smeared with molasses. Once placed outside, the prisoner's head would be invaded by flies and other insects.[67]

In 1861, legislation was passed to authorize the state's first prison, the Kansas State Penitentiary (KSP), to be located in Leavenworth County at Lansing, Kansas. At the time, there were twenty-one state prisoners, all being housed in the Leavenworth County Jail. While the Civil War delayed the construction of the prison for three years, the number of state prisoners began to steadily increase. By early 1864, the number of state prisoners had reached ninety, so many of them were removed from the overcrowded Leavenworth Jail and placed in the jail in Lawrence, Kansas.[68]

In the summer of 1864, construction of the state prison finally got underway with the building of a wooden barracks to house 100 prisoners. It was built by prisoners, most receiving sixty cents per day for their labor, while the state paid up to sixty-five cents per day for the board and care of these convicts. Within two years, the structure became overcrowded, holding 150 convicts. The tremendous increase in the state prison population was a phenomenon experienced around the country after the Civil War, as former soldiers increased prison populations. Ultimately, limestone cell houses would be constructed, and the first prisoners were transferred to the prison in July 1868.[69]

By 1875, there were 379 prisoners confined, 30 of whom were serving federal sentences. Four years later, an underground coal-mining operation was underway just outside the prison enclosure. The idea for a mine came from the notion that inmates needed labor to consume idle time. But this motive was only half of the equation. A more important goal was to provide labor opportunities that cultivate useful work skills while making the prison as financially self-sufficient as possible. At KSP, all convicts were expected to work in the coal mines, and the use of inmate labor earned a substantial amount of money for the state coffers. By 1890, inmates at KSP were producing 1.6 million bushels of coal, the sales amounting to $68,013.30.[70] Warden Codding had this to say about the relationship between inmate labor and revenue generated by the coal mines:

> *We should take more interest in the prisoner and less from him by making his education and improvement the paramount object of his imprisonment, instead of figuring how much work he can be made to do, how much coal he can mine and what he will produce. Especially should the young men be given individual treatment and instruction instead of being handled as a part of the mass. The mass handling of the men should give way to the individual management of each worthy prisoner.*[71]

Although Warden Codding argued that educating prisoners should be of primary concern, KSP continued to emphasize prisoner labor, in essence following national resolutions from the American Prison Association, which mandated that "the maintenance of all penal institutions, above the county jail, should be from the earnings of their inmates, and without cost to the state."

John Reynolds, a prisoner at the Kansas State Penitentiary in 1887, spent the first six months of a sixteen-month sentence working in the coal mines. He criticized the moral atmosphere of the mining operations in the following way:

> *The mines of this Penal institution are a college for the education and graduation of hardened criminals, and for illustration, and the instruction of those not familiar with the subject matter referred to, I will relate what came under my personal observation, and some things that I heard while in there. One day, in company with me while engaged in mining, were two other convicts. One of these was a hardened old crook. He was serving out a term on the charge of making and passing counterfeit money. The other fellow-convict was a young man seventeen years of age—a mere boy. Tired of mining, we laid off awhile, resting. During this time the old convict gave us instructions in the manner of making counterfeit money. He told us how he would construct his counterfeit molds out of plaster paris, which he would use in the same manner that bullet molds are used. He would purchase some britannica metal. On some dark night he would go into the forest, build up a fire, melt the metal, pour the melted liquor into the molds, and in this manner make silver dollars. He informed us that it didn't take very long to make a hatful of money. A few days thereafter this young man, who was with us in the room at the time, informed me that when he went out again into the world, if he was unable to secure work, he would try his hand at making counterfeit money. I advised him not to do this, as it was almost a certainty that he would be detected. He thought differently. About a month thereafter he was released from the prison. He went out into the world, and, unable to obtain work, DID try his hand at making counterfeit money. Shortly before my time expired here came this young man to prison again, with a sentence of three years at hard labor for making and passing counterfeit money. He had received his criminal instruction in the penitentiary mines, the result of which will be that he will spend the greater portion of his life a convict.*[72]

Along with the coal mine, the Kansas State Penitentiary employed prisoners in a brick factory and a twine mill. Bricks sold for $10.00 per thousand, and lime used in brick making sold for $0.35 a bushel. In 1870, the prison sold 3,018 bushels of lime and 32,100 bricks. The price of twine made at the penitentiary was always 1 cent per pound lower than that of trade brands. Prisoners were consistently paid a low wage, usually 3.75 cents per day.[73] So, using prison labor created the benefit of producing much-needed supplies at lower prices for Kansans while keeping the prisoners

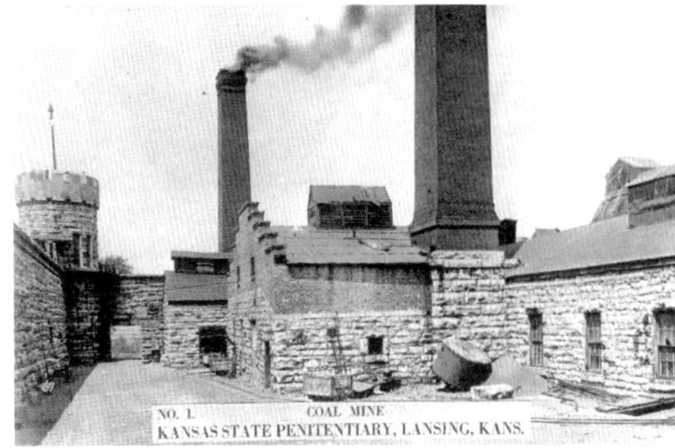

Left: Coal mine at the Kansas State Penitentiary, Lansing, Kansas, 1879. *Kansas Historical Society.*

Below: U.S. Disciplinary Barracks, Fort Leavenworth, Kansas.

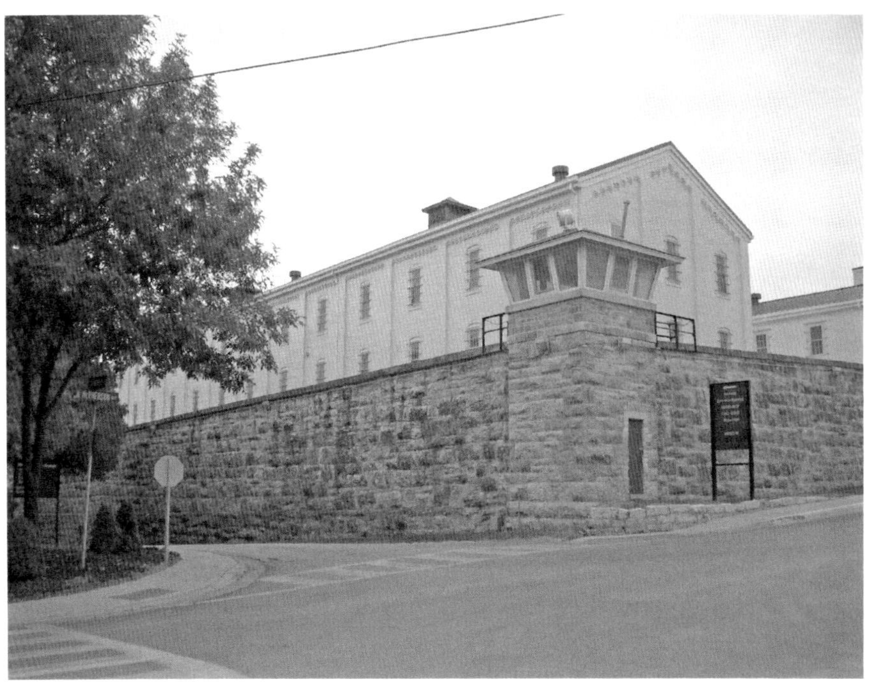

busy. But producing cheaply made goods undercut free labor and private business.[74] Laws would eventually be passed that regulated prison labor and the selling of goods for profit. By 1892, nearly one thousand prisoners called the Kansas State Penitentiary home, many of whom were prisoners on contract from the territory of Oklahoma.[75]

In addition to the Leavenworth city and county jails and the Kansas State Penitentiary, a military prison operated at Fort Leavenworth. The first buildings of the military prison were constructed in 1874, and it opened in 1875. Prior to that time, military offenders were confined in thirty-two

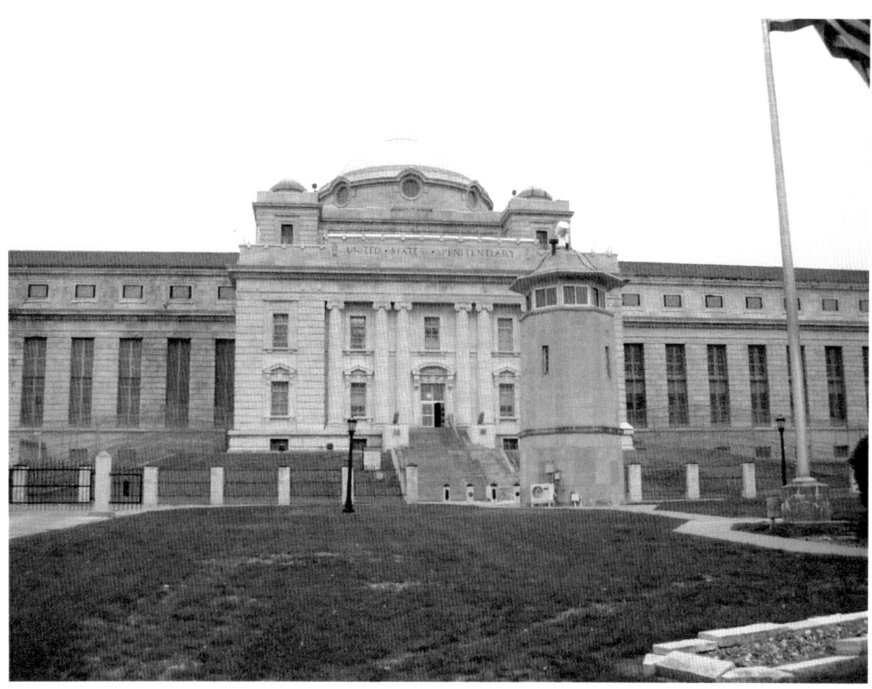

U.S. Penitentiary, Leavenworth, Kansas.

different stockade forts across the states and territories.[76] The treatment of these prisoners varied and included the use of ball and chain, shackling, solitary confinement and execution. In 1877, officials at the military prison began a vocational program that allowed prisoners to manufacture boots and shoes. A year later, the prison shoe factory was producing 150 pairs of shoes per day. Over the years, prisoners would also make soap, raise cattle and hogs and make tents.

But controversy over the exploitation of prison labor and the increased number of federal prisoners in the West led Congress to pass the Three Prison Act of 1891, effectively transferring jurisdiction of the military prison from the U.S. War Department to the U.S. Justice Department. As a result, the first federal penitentiary was built in Leavenworth. Shortly after the construction of the U.S. Penitentiary at Leavenworth, the army changed the name of the military prison to the United States Disciplinary Barracks and returned to "guardhouse" confinement, with the more serious offenders sent to Alcatraz or the state penitentiary.[77]

5

FIRST TERRITORIAL JAIL?

While Leavenworth continued to grow in population and reputation, other frontier settlements were developing to the south, as the California Road and Westport branch of the Santa Fe Trail passed through the northeastern corner of Johnson County, Kansas, and continued westward. Within this geographical area, the townships of Shawnee, originally known as Gum Springs, and Monticello are important to the history of Kansas jails during the early settlement period.

One of earliest settlements in Kansas, Shawnee Township is named for the Shawnee Indian reservation that was established through a series of treaties in the 1820s and 1830s. The reservation originally included a deed for 1,600,000 acres of land in eastern Kansas, including Johnson County. The Shawnee numbered only about nine hundred, including not more than twenty white men, who had intermarried into the tribe, which meant that 1,700 acres could be allotted to each member of the tribe.[78] But the westward push destined the need for land for white settlers in the region. For the Shawnee Township, it meant steady growth in land squatters at the expense of the Indians. In 1854, the Shawnee ceded to the United States all of the reservation but 200,000 acres, which they reserved for homes for themselves.[79]

Settlers encroaching on the territory cut timber for homes, plowed fields and claimed other natural resources. Sometimes these incoming home seekers were legal tenants, having bought land from the government. Every so often, though, they were illegal trespassers on government land. At the time, the U.S. marshals were the only law enforcement organization in the unorganized territory of Kansas. While protecting government property was of particular concern to the U.S. marshals, they did enforce all laws and pursued outlaws as directed by the federal courts. These lawmen would require a jail to detain prisoners, and the Shawnee Township would be as proper a place as any other to build a jail.

U.S. Marshals During the Kansas Territorial Period: 1854–1860

Marshal	Date
Donaldson, J.B.	June 29, 1854
Spencer, William	November 29, 1856
Dennis, Elias S.	March 12, 1857
Winston, Isaac	March 1, 1858
Fain, William P.	June 16, 1858
Colby, Philip T.	February 3, 1859

Miscellaneous notes, writings and news clippings point to the existence of a territorial jail in Shawnee as early as 1843.[80] The so-called Gum Springs Jail is reported to have been a one-story structure made of rough-faced stone, with wood shingles on the front elevation and a gabled roof.[81] The building design was symmetrical, with equally sized windows on both sides of a central single door. Photographs of the building over the years show the original structure bore a white sign above the door that read: "FIRST JAIL HOUSE, Territory of Kansas, 1843, The Jail Builder Was the First Offender." Supposedly, the jail stood for 125 years, until it was dismantled and rebuilt in Old Shawnee Town, an outdoor museum re-creating a Kansas prairie town dating from the 1840s to 1920s. However, while this building was commonly believed to be a territorial jail built in 1843, very little documented evidence existed to support that thought. An article published by the *Shawnee Journal Herald* newspaper in 1986 about the old jail and a house in the township noted, "At present, data at hand simply aren't complete enough to put a firm date on the house or the jail. It is just barely possible that they were built before 1857, but far more likely that they were built after that date."[82] In more recent years, research reports provided by architectural firms suggest that the jail building had been a house or a storefront.[83]

While the accuracy of the local legend has been called into question, and some have suggested that no such jail ever stood, it seems plausible that a U.S. marshal's office existed in the Kansas Territory during this time period.

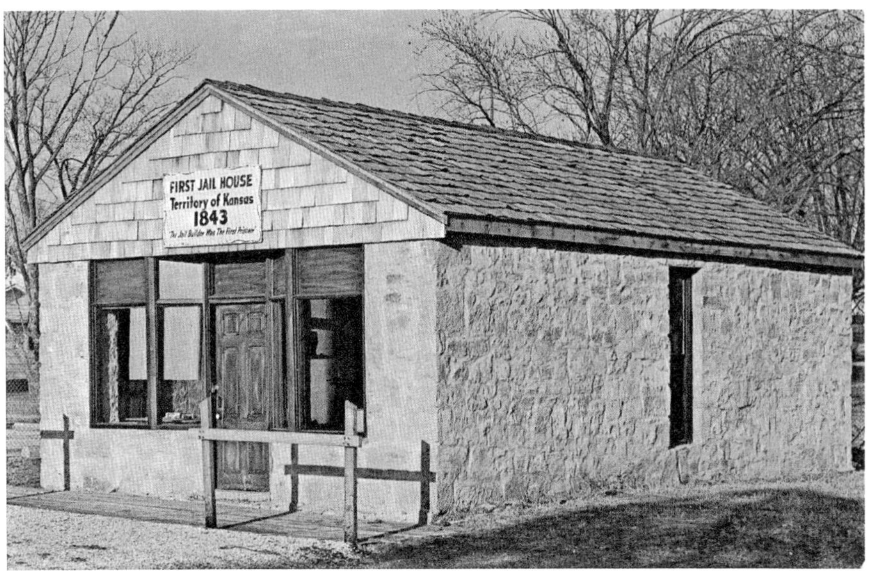

Purported first jail (1843) in Kansas Territory at Gum Springs, Kansas.

Such a place would have been necessary to serve as the headquarters of federal law enforcement officers and likely had a holding cell to temporarily quarter lawbreakers. The need for a jail was of particular concern after the passage of the Fugitive Slave Act of 1850, as the law enforcement arm of the federal judiciary was heavily involved with enforcing this act. Marshals were required to enforce the law, and any negligence in doing so exposed them to severe financial penalties. Any U.S. marshal who refused to act under the law was fined $1,000, and any person "obstructing arrest of [said] fugitive, harboring fugitives, or concealing them" was fined up to $1,000 and could serve up to six months in prison.[84]

In terms of understanding how seriously U.S. marshals took this directive, consider the fate of U.S. deputy marshal Leonard Arms. In 1856, John Ritchie, an abolitionist from Indiana, was arrested with thirteen others for "mail robbery" and confined at Fort Titus, a proslavery stronghold in Lecompton, Kansas Territory. He shortly thereafter escaped and fled back to Indiana to avoid the warrant issued for his arrest. In 1857, a general amnesty agreement was struck between proslavery forces and free-state men, whereby it was mutually agreed that charges against Ritchie and other free-state men should be dismissed. However, on August 20, 1860, Deputy Marshal Leonard Arms attempted to arrest forty-five-year-old Ritchie on the original warrant. Arms had developed a reputation for being a "slave catcher," and antislavery activists had warned

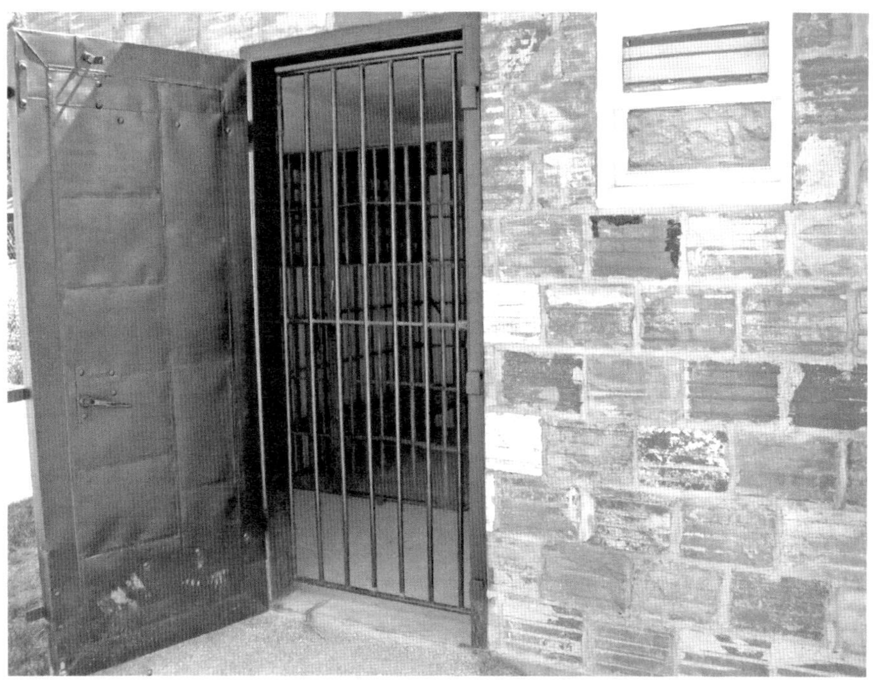

Above: Replica of the 1929 jail at the Shawnee Town Museum, Shawnee, Kansas.

Right: Iron cage inside the jail at the Shawnee Town Museum, Shawnee, Kansas.

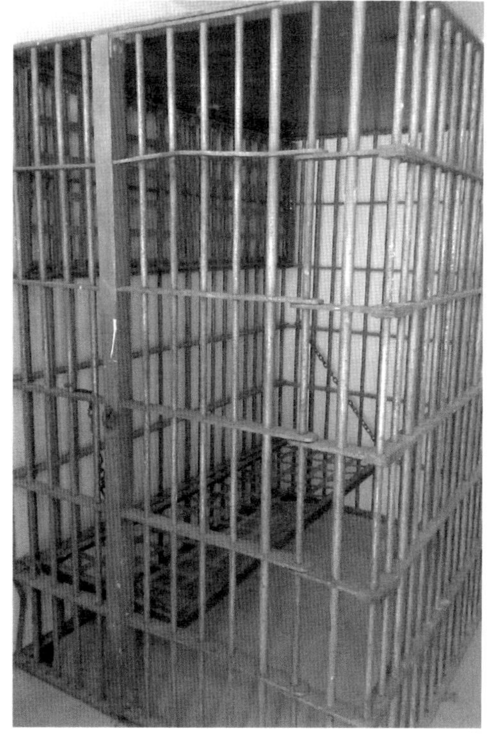

residents that Arms was particularly notorious for seizing runaway slaves and anyone helping them flee slavery.[85] When Ritchie refused to be arrested, Arms drew a revolver from his breast pocket and said, "Life is dear to me, but you will have to shoot quicker than I can if you kill me."[86] Ritchie retreated into his home and produced a pistol of his own; the two men were now armed and confronted each other. Ritchie fired once, fatally shooting Arms in the neck. He then fled but later in the evening surrendered himself to Justice C. Miller. Ritchie was charged with murder, and a trial was held the very next day. Justice Miller handed down his decision: "John Ritchie has committed homicide, but one justifiable in the sight of God and man. This being my honest conviction, the court deems it to be its duty to acquit the prisoner at the bar, charged with the murder of Leonard Arms, and discharge him from the custody of the law."[87]

So what about a city or county jail? It is unlikely that a local jail would have been built in the area until sometime after 1855, when the first territorial legislature established Johnson County as one of the original thirty-three counties in the territory. At the time, Shawnee Township (Gum Springs) was the original county seat, and some accounts of the period indicate that individuals were transported to Lecompton to be jailed. In 1856, for example, Calvin Cornatzer, a farmer residing just west of Shawnee Township, was arrested by Johnson County sheriff Isaac Parish and confined in the Lecompton jail for one day for aiding and abetting the free-state cause.[88] It is even more unlikely that a jail was ever built in Shawnee during the 1800s because the township lost its designation as county seat. In 1858, Olathe became incorporated as a city and designated as the county seat the following year. According to the history of Johnson County, Colonel Josiah E. Hayes was hired in 1858 to build "the new county jail, at a cost of $6,000, and he built and delivered it to the county the same year, and it remained a serviceable building [in Olathe] until destroyed by fire in 1905."[89]

That being said, Shawnee's first city jail may have not been built until 1926, when a small, square building was constructed to house prisoners. The exterior of the jail was made of red terra-cotta tile blocks. The interior of the jail contained two cells measuring five by seven feet each.[90] According to an article in the *Johnson County Democrat* newspaper:

> *The city jail…sits like a spider in its web waiting for a fly, awaiting the first victim which to date, has not been forthcoming. The jail…has been built entirely from fines collected from motorists passing through Shawnee since the hard surfaced road has been opened for careless driving, speeding, driving a car while intoxicated and too often for no cause at all.*[91]

6

CONSTABLE JAMES BUTLER HICKOK

In 1857, several townships were established in Johnson County, Kansas, including the small township of Monticello, just eight miles southeast of Shawnee. Monticello was platted at the crossroads of the east–west Midland trail from Westport to Lawrence and the military road from Fort Leavenworth to Fort Scott, Kansas. By 1858, the town's population had swelled to 1,250 pioneers, frontiersmen and immigrants. Local law enforcement was provided by the territorial sheriff, Pat Cosgrove, and his deputy, Samuel Wear. In March 1858, four constables were hired to enforce the law in Monticello, including James Butler Hickok, popularly known a few years later as Wild Bill. While much has been written about Hickok, the following depiction of the man is perhaps as accurate as any posed: "Wild Bill was generous to a fault, swore like a trooper at certain stages, and would rather indulge in poker than eat, on one occasion having played away his last earthly possession, a black and tan terrier."[92]

Hickok was only twenty years old when he took on the first of several law enforcement jobs in Kansas. The few surviving records from that era reveal that Hickok was one of the arresting officers in the first murder trial in Johnson County. Newspaper stories also tell of young Hickok recovering twenty-five stolen horses, serving several summonses and quelling a brawl or two during his term.[93]

Hickok would leave Monticello after only a little more than a year but meandered throughout Kansas for most of his life.[94] His jobs were short term, and several included being a lawman in Kansas cowtowns, including U.S. deputy marshal and special policeman (Hays, Kansas), sheriff (Ellis County, Kansas) and city marshal (Abilene, Kansas). While employed as city marshal of Abilene at a salary of $150 per month, Hickok spent much of his time at the Alamo Saloon, where he could be found gambling while on duty. If he was needed, his deputies knew where to find him, and when called on to act, Hickok thought nothing of running a disorderly cowboy out of town or locking him up in the Abilene jail.

One of the more tragic events involving Hickok was a shootout that was instigated by Phil Coe, the owner of the Bulls Head Saloon, and the accidental killing of Deputy Mike Williams. Coe was a reputed gunfighter and gambler who settled in Abilene in the spring of 1871. He and Hickok had a soured relationship, and when the two men started courting the same woman, rumors circulated that each planned to kill the other. On October 5, 1871, a number of Texas cowboys were celebrating the end of the cattle season by drinking in Abilene's many saloons. Working their way toward the Alamo Saloon, shots were fired, and Hickok emerged from the saloon to investigate the ruckus. Like many Kansas towns in the 1870s, Abilene had passed an ordinance prohibiting carrying firearms in the town. Seeing Coe in the mix with guns drawn, Hickok ordered him to surrender his firearms. Coe refused and instead fired two shots at Hickok, who promptly returned fire and killed Coe. Hickok was unharmed but alert and leery of others on the street who might be carrying guns. Mike Williams, a city jail officer, heard the shots and ran to the scene to assist Hickok. As Williams rounded the corner of a building, Hickok caught a glimpse of movement and fired in reaction, accidentally shooting Williams in the head.[95] He was the last man killed by the legendary Wild Bill.[96]

By the late 1870s, Hickok's days as a lawman were over, and he married Agnes Thatcher Lake in Cheyenne, Wyoming Territory. Hickok soon headed out for the gold fields of the Black Hills in the Dakota Territory, determined to earn enough money through prospecting and gambling to put his marriage on a sound financial base. But on August 2, 1876, at the age of thirty-nine, Hickok was shot to death by Jack McCall while playing poker in the Nuttal & Mann's Saloon No. 10 in Deadwood. The killing was apparently over McCall's drunken resentment of Hickok offering him money to buy breakfast after McCall had lost it all playing poker the previous day. McCall claimed, however, that the killing was retribution for Hickok

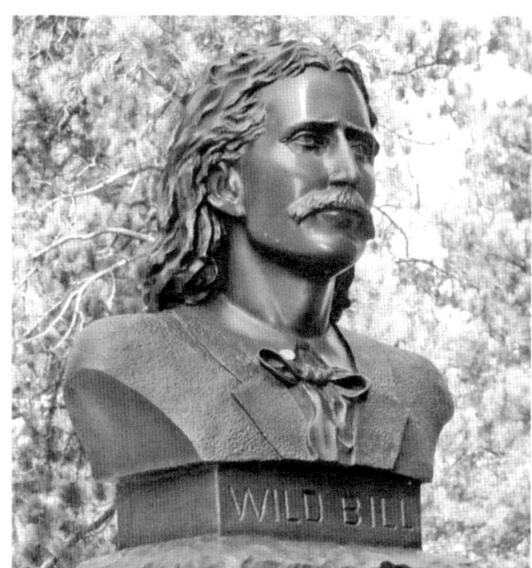

Right: Monument of James Butler "Wild Bill" Hickok in the Mount Moriah Cemetery, Deadwood, South Dakota.

Below: Mount Moriah Cemetery dedications to James Butler "Wild Bill" Hickok and Martha "Calamity Jane" Burke.

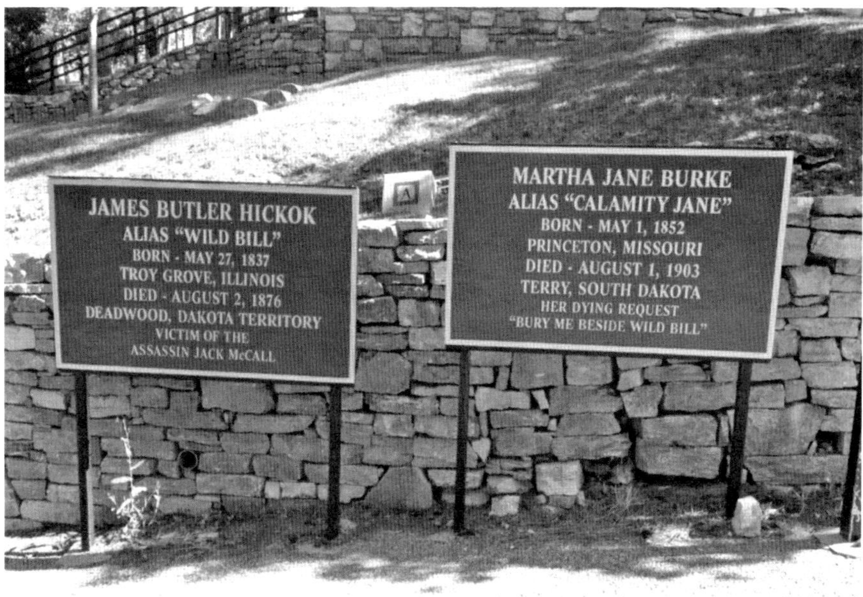

having previously killed McCall's brother in Abilene, Kansas. At the time of the murder, Hickok allegedly held a poker hand of two pair (aces and eights) forever known as the Dead Man's Hand.[97] Hickok was buried just south of Deadwood in an area known as Ingleside but later moved to Mount Moriah Cemetery in south Deadwood.[98]

Part III
AN INVITATION TO VIOLENCE

Pioneers heading west into Kansas Territory were looking for cheap, if not free, land to settle. The Preemption Act of 1841 permitted squatters to stake a claim of 160 acres of land and, after fourteen months of residence, purchase the land for $1.25 per acre. Unclaimed land was either sold by the federal government or given away to encourage westward expansion. As settlers moved in, towns, churches, saloons and stores were built, and communities flourished (albeit sometimes only briefly). Living in the Kansas Territory also meant dealing with the tense political situation that was brewing about the slave debate. The Kansas-Nebraska Act of 1854 had repealed the Missouri Compromise and introduced the principle of popular sovereignty. No longer would there be a prohibition on slavery in territories north of 36°30′ latitude. Instead, settlers would determine whether slavery would be allowed within the territories. While some settlers tried to remain neutral, the reality was they had to choose sides.

Historians agree that most white settlers who opposed the extension of slavery in the Kansas Territory originally hailed from states that protected the holding of black indentured servants (e.g., Illinois, Ohio). They opposed slavery not because they found enslavement morally wrong but because they harbored a strong desire for an all-white population.[99] These settlers, with their ethnocentric upbringing, "presumed that slavery was the prerequisite for a large free Negro population" and that the best means "of preventing the residence of free Negroes was to prohibit slavery."[100] Those who opposed slavery because it flooded the territory with blacks would join ranks with true abolitionists, who believed slavery was immoral and inherently unjust.

Combined, they formed the "free-staters" and would oppose the proslavery Missourians who wanted Kansas to be a slave state. Missourians living along the western border of the state were branded border ruffians, a label denoting them as marauding bushwhackers.

By the summer of 1854, many settlements had been founded by proslavery supporters along the Kansas River. The township of Lawrence, on the other hand, was established by abolitionists from Boston and became the launching point for antislavery emigrants to establish additional settlements, Topeka being one in early December 1854. Towns in eastern Kansas were the site of fierce and violent confrontations between men who would not compromise their views about whether the Kansas Territory should be a slave state. During the partisan violence years, 56 men died. The two sides were nearly equally involved in killing their political opponents: 30 proslavery people, 24 antislavery men, 1 officially neutral U.S. soldier and 1 man whose political persuasion is obscured by an imprecise historical record.[101] Bloody skirmishes fueled and extended the border war for many years, a firestorm before and during the Civil War. During the War Between the States, Kansas would suffer nearly 8,500 casualties—a remarkable showing for an infant state with only 30,000 men of military age.[102]

In and among the fighting between proslavery and antislavery settlers, a large number of men spent much of their time drinking and gambling and often engaged in public disorder. Many were arrested and charged with breach of peace, a violation of the public tranquility and order. Outlaws would also emerge that required the territory's lawmen to take action. Consequently, the building of jails became a priority to detain both proslavery and antislavery supporters, rabble and criminals alike. These buildings were anything but strongholds, and escapes were common. Jail space was much in demand, and additional jails would be needed as settlers pushed farther into the Kansas Territory.

7

THE GREAT POLITICAL PRISON HOME AT LECOMPTON

In the spring of 1855, the township of Lecompton became the capital of Kansas Territory. It was named in honor of Chief Justice Samuel LeCompte, a steadfast proslavery Democrat whose tenure on the bench largely coincided with the Bleeding Kansas period. Lecompton was the site of the first elections in the territory, and Constitution Hall became the seat of territorial government, as well as the office for filing land claims. It was here that the territorial legislature drafted the Lecompton Constitution to admit Kansas to the Union as a slave state. When the document was sent to Washington for ratification, it was rejected by the House, but not before it created deep wedges within the Democratic Party. The division led the Democrats to offer two candidates for president in 1860, which split the party vote, opening the way for Abraham Lincoln to win as a Republican with only 39 percent of the popular vote.

After completion of the original twenty-five- by thirty-four-foot Constitution Hall building, a two-story addition was added to the rear, extending the building to twenty-five by fifty feet. Historical photographs indicate that the building was slightly changed over the years, including adding entry porches and exterior stairs to the second floor. The first floor hosted hundreds of settlers who filed land claims. They sometimes resorted to bareknuckle fighting for their share of the rich lands that were opening for settlement. Upstairs, the U.S. District Court was regularly in session to enforce the territorial laws. Many free-state people refused to obey these laws because they had been passed by the proslavery territorial legislature. This resistance made law enforcement tough for territorial officials, and often U.S. Dragoon soldiers from Fort Leavenworth were summoned to help maintain order.

Many abolitionists were charged with various offenses and quickly found themselves as prisoners under guard in military-controlled encampments. In the spring of 1856, as many as six hundred U.S. troops set up an encampment three miles outside Lecompton. They named the field post Camp Sackett, after Captain Delos Sackett of the First Cavalry at Fort Leavenworth, and were charged with keeping the peace between free-state and proslavery militias. Throughout most of 1856, Camp Sackett became a place to confine prisoners and was used by Chief Justice LeCompte to confine five free-state men, who would be called the "treason prisoners." During that year, a grand jury issued indictments for treason against Charles Robinson, George Deitzler, Gaius Jenkins, George W. Brown and John Brown Jr., the eldest son of the famous abolitionist.[103] These free-state men were incarcerated at Camp Sackett. In July, Robinson wrote a letter to John C. Frémont, who was running as the first Republican nominee for president of the United States, using the political slogan: "Free soil, free labor, free speech, free men, Fremont." In the letter, Robinson commented on his imprisonment, writing, "Affairs here are as bad as they can be. Tyranny rules with a rod of iron….It is unknown as yet whether Pierce has fully decided to hang us or not. However, if our hanging can change this infernal administration they will not make much by the investment."[104] In September, the prisoners were arraigned for treason, granted $5,000 bail, had their new cases continued and were released. It was speculated that the reason Judge Lecompte granted a continuance was the looming arrival of the new Kansas territorial governor John Geary, who was sympathetic to the free-state cause and who would influence the trial in the defendants' favor. Ultimately, the treason charges were dropped against the defendants, and they were released in September 1856.

On January 29, 1861, Kansas was admitted to the Union as a free state, and Charles Robinson became the first governor of the state of Kansas. It was during Governor Robinson's four months of confinement at Camp Sackett that many of Bleeding Kansas's most violent incidents occurred: the sack of Lawrence, the Pottawatomie Massacre and the Battles of Black Jack and Osawatomie, to name just a few. In 1898, Robinson published a book titled *The Kansas Conflict*, dedicating the manuscript to Eli Thayer, the organizer of the Massachusetts Emigrant Aid Company, which sent hundreds of antislavery settlers to the Kansas Territory.[105]

Prisoners not finding themselves under military guard were confined in the Lecompton prison home, its name providing some indication of the structure of the jail and its original intended usage. In fact, while it has not been determined what building in Lecompton was the actual prison house, it is most likely the structure was one of several buildings owned by J.N.O.P. (Dr. John P.) Wood.

A dealer in dry goods, groceries, hardware, clothing and other materials, Dr. John Wood moved to Lecompton in March 1856. He was a physician by training but also held the dual offices of United States commissioner for Kansas Territory and probate judge in the proslavery government.[106] He arraigned many free-state defendants charged in territorial courts and, during 1856, confined them in a building he owned. In January 1858, Wood filed a claim for costs associated with boarding these prisoners.[107] This is one of the few claims filed for costs that fell into the "public" class, which required each claimant to submit an itemized list and have two witnesses attest to the losses claimed. A portion of Dr. Wood's claim included $4,642.75 for boarding on the following dates:[108]

September 22, 1856—boarding of 103 prisoners 4 days, at 75 cents per day…$299.00
September 26—boarding of 113 prisoners 10 days, at 75 cents per day…$846.50
October 6—boarding of 94 prisoners 15 days, at 75 cents per day…$1,057.50
October 21—boarding of 91 prisoners 16 days at 75 cents per day…$1,092.00
November 6—boarding of 87 prisoners 11 days at 75 cents per day…$ 717.75
November 17—boarding 84 prisoners 10 days at 75 cents per day…$630.00

One witness to Dr. Wood's claim was William P. Caldwell, a resident of Lecompton during the fall of 1856, who served as a militia man mustered into U.S. service to guard free-state prisoners. According to Caldwell's statement in support of the petition by John Wood:

> *These prisoners were kept in Doctor's Wood's house, now known as the National Hotel, in Lecompton; he supplied these prisoners with provisions, with stoves, fuel, beds and bedding, and clothing; these prisoners were kept in the house and supplied by Doctor Wood about three months; never knew any one else was able to furnish the provisions; Doctor Wood has a dry goods and grocery store; had a good stock of goods;…also a house for them to stay in during the time that these prisoners were kept in Lecompton.*[109]

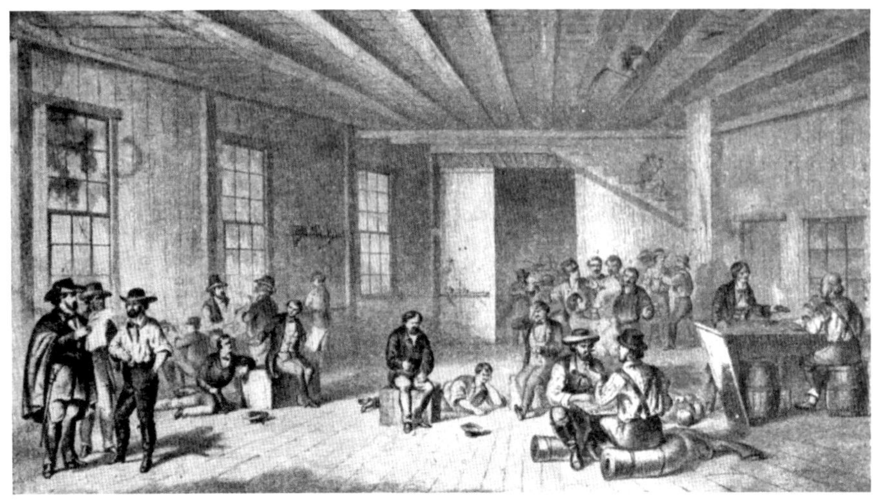

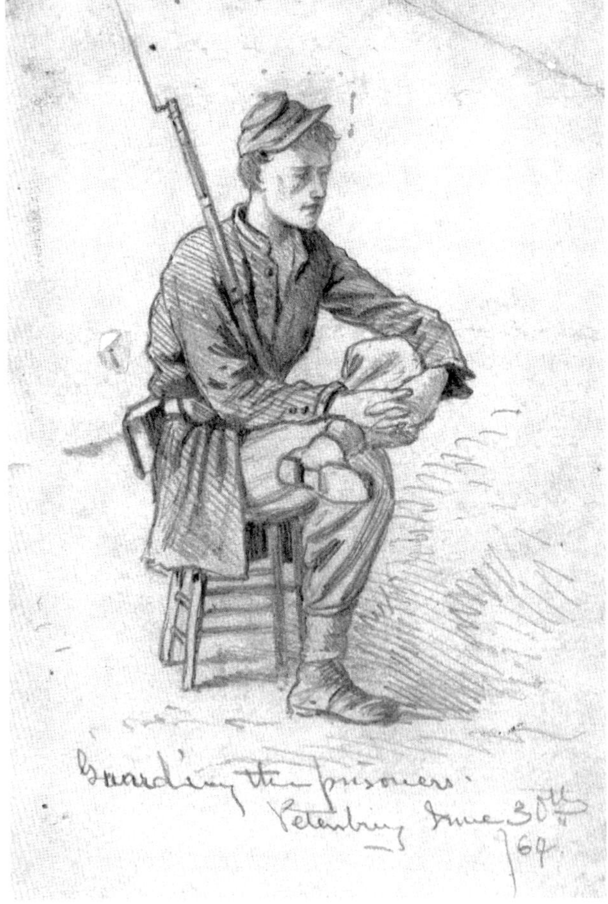

Above: Lithograph of Lecompton Prison: "Inside view of the lower prison at Lecompton." Sketch by William Breyman, circa 1860. *Lecompton Historical Society.*

Left: Drawing of a solider guarding the prisoners. *Library of Congress.*

The Lecompton Prison home was a typical residential building for the times, made of wood with glass windows and designed as a meeting place rather than a place of confinement. At best, it was a makeshift jail with very little in the way of amenities one might think would exist in a jail. Prisoners were left to congregate in an open room that featured no cells but relied on guards to hold the prisoners within the structure. The lithograph of Lecompton Prison (on page 66) is from a sketch by William Breyman, who was a farmer in Kansas.[110] In 1856, Breyman participated in the Battle of Hickory Point and was captured along with 101 antislavery prisoners, charged with murder in the first degree and imprisoned at Lecompton.[111]

There is a recounting from a southern man who, shortly after arriving in Lecompton, asked the territorial governor to see the robbers and murderers taken into custody and jailed. The governor approved the visit to the prison home and assured him that by paying it a visit, he might gratify his curiosity. After reaching the described location and looking in vain for anything that resembled a prison, he approached two men, who were engaged in a game of quoits (horseshoes). Their conversation went as follows:

> *"Can you tell me, where the prison is in which those great robbers and murderers are confined?"*
>
> *"That's it," said one of the men, pointing to a house near at hand.*
>
> *"What! That old building, falling to pieces, without either doors or windows? You don't want to tell me that they keep murderers and thieves and other criminals there?"*
>
> *"That is the only prison we have here," replied the man, deliberately pitching his quoit.*
>
> *"Well," says the southern gentleman, "I want to see those desperate murderers and assassins."*
>
> *"I am one of them," says the quoit–player, "and that is another," pointing to his companion.*
>
> *"What! You convicted felons? You the terrible murderers about whom I have heard so much?"*
>
> *"Yes; we are certainly two of them. The others are gone over to the House of Representatives, to hear the members abuse the governor."*
>
> *"But," says the old gentleman, "They don't allow convicted murderers to go about in this way, without a guard to watch them?"*
>
> *"Oh, yes," says the man interrogated; "they used to send a guard with us, whenever we went over to the Legislative Halls, to protect us against violence from the members; but they found that too troublesome and*

expensive; so they gave each of us a revolver and bowie–knife, and told us we should hereafter be required to protect ourselves."

"But why don't you run away? You have every opportunity. There is nothing to prevent you."

"Why, to tell the truth, we have often been persuaded to do that; but then, you see these rascally legislators have been threatening to assassinate the governor, and we have determined to remain here to watch them, and protect him."[112]

Several events occurred at the Lecompton Prison home that ultimately prompted talk of constructing an actual jail building. One incident occurred on September 27, 1856, when Charles Calkins, a convicted prisoner, threw a blanket over his head and shoulders and walked out of the prison unnoticed by the guards. A requisition for troops was made by the master of convicts, and a reward of $100 was proffered by the governor for the "escapee's" capture, but without success.[113]

The position of master of convicts had been established in 1855, when territorial statutes were enacted by the governor and legislative assembly. Chapter 22 of the statutes, titled "Confinement and Hard Labor," specified that a master of convicts would be commissioned by the governor to take charge and control of convicts and employ guards as necessary to ensure that convicts completed hard labor at public works sites. The master of convicts was paid $2.50 per day, and guards were paid $1.50 per day. Convicts engaged in hard labor were to be securely confined by a six-foot-long chain with a round ball of iron of not less than four to six inches in diameter. Another provision of the act vacated the position of the master of convicts once a penitentiary was built.[114] In 1856, Governor John Geary appointed Levi J. Hampton as the first master of convicts in the Kansas Territory.[115] A few months later, Hampton submitted his first official report. A portion of this report provides some insight into the difficulties of the job and Hampton's plea for the legisture to appropriate funds for a penitentiary:

On entering upon the duties of my office, there were reported to me twenty-two convicts, in charge of Colonel Titus, then in command of the territorial militia. They remained in that position up to the 25th of November, at which time eighteen were handed over to me, four having previously escaped from prison (referring to the Lecompton prison home). One of the eighteen has since escaped from my custody. He has not yet been recaptured, although every effort has been made to retake him...

> *The fact of there being no place of safe confinement, or means placed at my disposal for their security, as the law requires, these prisoners are, to some extent, at large. I have endeavored to have them properly guarded. It is however, a matter beyond all controversy, that the proper punishment for crime, and the consequent protection of life and property, demand the speedy erection of a penitentiary.*[116]

It wasn't until February 1858 that Kansas Territory acting governor J.W. Denver signed into law an act concerning county jails that every county would be required to establish a jail at the expense of the county—"for the safe-keeping of prisoners lawfully committed." The sheriff of the county, by himself or with a deputy, "shall keep the jail, and shall be responsible for the manner in which the same is kept. He shall keep separate rooms for the sexes, except where they are lawfully married. He shall supply bread, meat, drink and fuel for the prisoners."[117]

A second event occurred in October that furthered public outcry to do something about the prison home. A *New York Tribune* reporter visited Lecompton and described it this way:

> *Yesterday, I visited the prisoners at Lecompton. It was my second visit to that forlorn town....Instead of the rising schoolhouses and churches of Lawrence, the little street is lined with barrooms....Southern provincialisms strike one's ears at every moment and the town is garrisoned by...militia, reinforced yesterday by 25 precious youths from Georgia, in a high state of whiskey. They were very visible, being allowed an area of a square rod or so before their prison door, guarded by a few young Missourians who pace up and down with loaded muskets....The prisoners lounged about looking as prisoners everywhere do. They are kept in a large unfinished wooden building, without an atom of furniture. They do their own cooking with very scanty utensils. They have obtained with great difficulty 15 straw pallets. Some have no blankets. It was an extremely cold windy day when I was there; the exposed side of the house was unfinished, and about half its superficial extent consisted of great gaps through which the wind whistled. A few men lay about on the floor sick with fever and ague. Most of them are young men.*[118]

A few months later, prisoners removed a portion of the stovepipe, and a fire broke out on the building's roof. Although the flames were extinguished before the jail incurred too much damage, it became obvious that a real jail was needed in the territorial capital. Three days later, the *Kansas Weekly Herald* published a notice that the board of commissioners of Douglas County would accept sealed bids through December 1, 1856, for the building of a county jail at Lecompton—the cost not to exceed $5,000.[119]

While Lecompton would continue to grow in population, a permanent county jail would not be built in this town during the territorial years. In 1857, free staters were elected for the first time to the majority in the territorial legislature, and they quickly voted to move the seat of Douglas County from the proslavery stronghold of Lecompton to Lawrence, the headquarters of the free-state movement. In January 1858, the county seat was permanently moved to Lawrence. It was not until 1892 that a jail would be built in Lecompton, Kansas. This jail was constructed of native limestone and wood, measuring seven feet by nine feet on the inside and eleven feet by thirteen feet on the outside. Its walls were two feet thick, with hand-forged iron window bars. The jail was used into the 1920s and relocated in 2012 through efforts of the Lecompton Historical Society and Douglas County Heritage Conservation Council.

8

THE IRON JAIL OF LAWRENCE CITY

While a courthouse would not be built in Lawrence until the early 1900s, the first jail was built in 1857.[120] At a cost of $800, the building was a twenty- by twenty-foot hewn log structure used to temporarily confine prisoners. Soon after its completion, a prisoner escaped, with the help of a friend, by cutting a hole through the roof.[121] A more permanent Douglas County Jail for the new county seat in Lawrence was conceived in 1858 and became the first public structure designed by John Haskell, well known for having designed many important buildings in Kansas, including the east wing of the Kansas Statehouse, courthouses, university buildings, government buildings, schools, churches, hospitals and opera houses.[122] Materials for the jail took three years to be delivered by steamboat up the Kaw River. The delay in the delivery of iron materials that would be necessary to build the jail was caused by the drought of 1860. Low water in the river meant that steamers could deliver their iron cargo only as far as the township of Desoto, some twenty miles away. The materials for the jail were afterward hauled on wagons to Lawrence.[123]

At an estimated cost of $18,000, the Douglas County Jail finally opened sometime between 1859 and 1861.[124] It was constructed by Enoch Jacobs Foundry of Cincinnati, Ohio, an ironworks company that made jail cells, stairs and general metal products. Jacobs's patents illustrate the kind of jail equipment he made and included:

Jail and Prison	No. 24,307	Patented June 7, 1859
Prison Door Fastening	No. 26,108	Patented November 15, 1859
Iron Plate Jail	No. 26,500	Patented December 20, 1859
Metallic Plate Joint	No. 27,222	Patented February 21, 1860
Lock	No. 43,915	Patented August 23, 1864

The Douglas County Jail was dubbed the first iron jail built in the West and considered the strongest structure of its kind in the Kansas Territory. Criminals were often brought to the jail from "some weaker jail, to be kept in safety from the mobs that craved vengeance."[125] This two-story jail comprised double rows of cells arranged with masonry walls enclosing the cells and access to the cells through grated doors. The cells were made of angle iron and cement and arranged in rows, with an end of each facing a surrounding gallery. The opposite end of each cell faced a central passage, which extended the whole length of the row of cells and was wide enough to afford space for ventilator flues and soil ducts. One of the goals of the design was to allow guards the opportunity to eavesdrop on the prisoners "for the purpose of overhearing and detecting conspiracies among them, or any attempts that they may be making to escape."[126] There was no water and no sewerage in the jail, and the jailer was forced to have prisoners carry in water and coal by tubs.

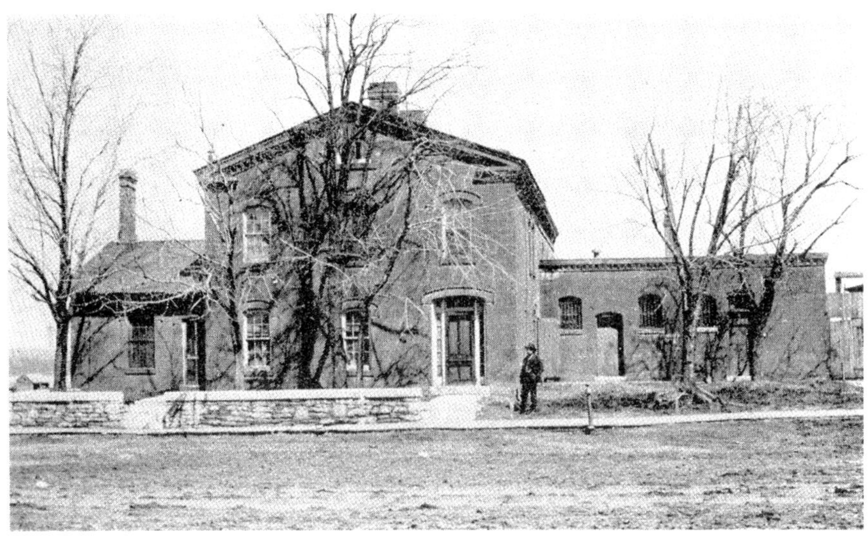

Douglas County Jail in 1898 after sections had been constructed on both sides of the original jail. *Douglas County Historical Society, Watkins Museum of History.*

Although its capacity was limited to forty prisoners, the jail often accommodated as many as sixty. Some of these prisoners were from other towns that had yet to construct a jail building. Consider the following newspaper editorial by Jacob Stotler to the residents of Emporia, Kansas, in May 1862:

> *The subject of building a jail in this county is now being somewhat agitated. Whatever may be said about the matter, pro or con, the county certainly needs such an institution, as a matter of economy. At present we have a prisoner charged with the crime of murder, who has been in the hands of the sheriff for a week, and has to be kept at the hotel at an expense of $3.50 to $4.00 per week, and attended by a guard constantly....The nearest jail is at Lawrence, and if evil-doers in this county are to be placed in dungeons, they have to be taken there, where the cash is demanded every week in advance for keeping him.*[127]

Hangings took place sometimes within the Lawrence jail, as was the case in the first execution that occurred in 1865, "when an Indian and a white man were hung according to the law."[128] The next and most fateful hanging took place on June 10, 1882, when a large mob of angry white men broke into the jail and took three black prisoners in order to hang them. Peter Vinegar, George Robertson and Ike King had been found guilty of bludgeoning to death David Bausman, a native of Ohio who had been in Lawrence to visit his brother. The three murderers were taken to the iron wagon bridge over the Kansas River, a short distance from the jail. Some of the lynch mob wore scarves around their faces; others had covered their faces with wood ash. The sheriff did little to try to stop the lynching. The arms of the prisoners had been restrained and the ropes adjusted about their necks before leaving the jail. Upon reaching the middle span of the bridge, Robertson's rope was secured to the ironwork. A dozen strong arms lifted him from his feet and dropped him over, but in doing so, the rope binding his arms became unfastened; reaching up, he caught hold of the rope that was about his neck and tried to save himself, making his death slow and painful. Vinegar followed and died without a struggle. The last to be hanged was King, saying, "Boys, let me down easy." They did, and he died slowly, strangling to death. The bodies were cut down and placed in the jail yard.[129]

The jail would serve Douglas County for more than fifty years and was dismantled in 1918. According to Isaac "Ike" Johnson, a jailer who had

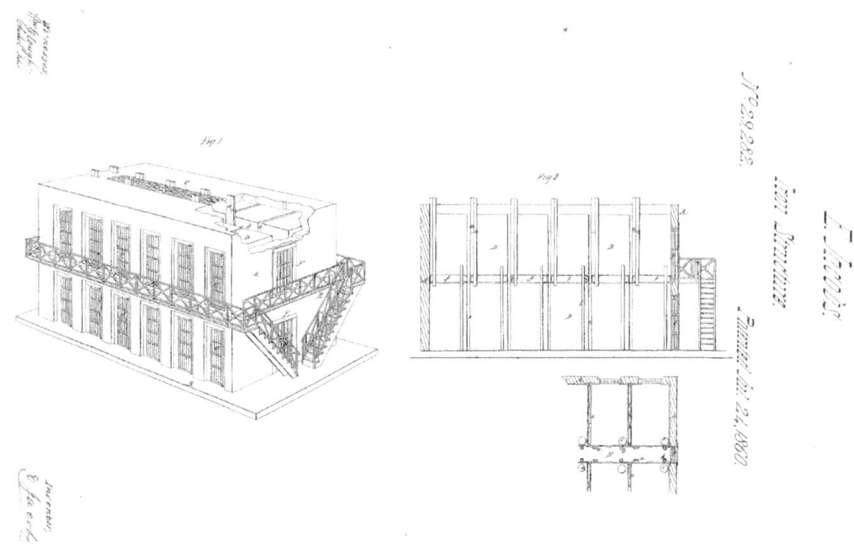

Schematic drawing of iron plate jail cells in Lawrence, Kansas. *U.S. Patent and Trademark Office.*

worked in the building since 1888, "many of the jailers were knocked in the head" by prisoners attempting to escape. Apparently, this occurred because the jailers were locked inside with the prisoners. Mr. Johnson was a well-known character of Lawrence for many years, distinguishing himself for faithful service as turnkey for the county.[130] "The worst prisoners I ever had in jail," said Johnson,

> *were three fellows awaiting trial. Two of them had robbed a hardware store and the third was a horse thief. Those three men made several attempts to saw their way to liberty, but each time some other prisoner gave me the tip and I went after their saws. One of them had an axe, with which he intended to kill me in the delivery if I made a move to stop them. I never carry a pistol in the cell room. I never give a bad man that much advantage over me. They would disarm me in a minute and that would be my end.*[131]

9

MOBOCRACY

The hanging of Peter Vinegar, George Robertson and Ike King is just one example of frontier justice at the hands of a lynch mob. There were many such occurrences in frontier Kansas, some arising out of a need for vengeance and others from a rampant desire to "do something" when the law was either ineffective or didn't exist. Mob justice grew more and more pervasive in towns like Lawrence, as the fear of being bushwhacked and murdered gave acceptance to the notion that such criminals deserved the violent response of the forces of law and order, whether that be a judicial order from a court or the dictate of an angry mob.

The history of mobocracy in the early days of Kansas tells us that the difference between a lynching and a legal hanging was quite often a matter of personal opinion and the consensus of the citizens. So, a mob hanging could be seen as a virtuous and lawful act by some while sinful and unjust by others. Consider, for example, the fate of Thomas Corlew, a carpenter from Missouri, who was hanged as a spy for Confederate guerrilla leader William Clarke Quantrill. Corlew, also known as John Calloo, and two brothers came to the Kansas Territory in 1854 and were known to the people of Lawrence as being proslavery supporters. On August 22, 1863, the day after Quantrill's Raid on Lawrence, Corlew was taken into custody and immediately given a jury trial. He was found guilty, and a vote was taken to hang him. James C. Horton, who served in the Kansas House of Representatives in 1874 and in the Kansas Senate in 1875 and 1876, wrote concerning the event:

> *I was there during the whole proceeding and went to one or two parties whom I thought might stop it, but to no avail. My recollection is that the jury did not find any evidence against him and so reported. His hanging was perhaps a natural outcome of the excited state of public feeling at that time, as Corlew was a Missourian and was said to have been acting with the proslavery men in 1856, but I think that many people in Lawrence regretted the occurrence and in ordinary, quiet times no such termination of a trial, even by a lynch court, would have been permitted.*[132]

Another reason for the prevalence of mob justice was that escapes from jails happened on a regular basis. The one sure thing we know about frontier jails is that as soon as someone claimed that the jail was escape-proof, a prisoner would stroll contentedly out the front door. Escapes sometimes had to do with flaws in the building. One of the best illustrations of this occurred in Seneca, the county seat of Nemaha County, Kansas. In 1861, citizens built the city's first jail, a twenty- by thirty-foot stone building that "allowed tenants to escape easily."[133] County commissioners would approve a new fifty-two- by thirty-two-foot, one-story brick jail, which opened in 1879. Unfortunately, not long after it was constructed, prisoners escaped by digging up the sand and brick flooring and tunneling out of the structure. By the turn of the century, general deterioration had weakened the building so much that, on one occasion, a prisoner simply pushed out a section of a wall and walked out of the jail. Jailbreaks became commonplace, causing the editor of the local newspaper to write, "There has been some eight or ten jail escapes since the jail has been in use, and several important criminals have got away."[134] After a total renovation in 1907, including re-bricking the entire building, the structure was once again solid and remained functional for seventy more years.

More often than not, escapes had less to do with the building's design and structure and more to do with the role of the jail keeper. Some jailers were overpowered by inmates and had no help available to them. Certainly, the chance of escape increased for prisoners when the jailer was negligent about his duties. Worse yet were those times when the jailer decided that a little bribe wouldn't hurt anyone. Considering that a jailer earned about seventy-five cents per day to oversee the jail operation, it often proved profitable to go in cahoots with the prisoners and wander away from the jail for a short time so that a jailbreak could happen.

The list of incidents underscoring the degree to which mob justice occurred throughout frontier Kansas is large. In 1870, for example, a vigilante group of cattlemen formed to put an end to a horse theft operation in south-central

Kansas. A local paper published the vigilantes' warning: "They had killed four [horse thieves] on November 4th and four on December 4th, and that they proposed to kill four on the 4th of every month thereafter until all were gone, and that any attempt to prosecute them therefore, meant death." It was signed "798 Vigilantes."[135] As another example of violence begetting violence, consider the mob lynching of three men in Parker, Kansas. These men were arrested for murder and locked up in the city jail. At around 3:30 a.m. on February 8, 1871, about fifty vigilantes overtook the jailers and promptly hanged the three prisoners from a nearby oak tree. Two weeks later, a local newspaper expressed this perspective when, in decrying the violent actions of a lynch mob in Parker, Kansas, it explained: "Mob law is unjustifiable in a settled country like that which surrounds Parker where courts of justice are in full and successful operations."[136]

Whether extralegal punishment was imposed by a group of Kansas cattlemen or some other vigilante group, lynch mobs existed because of the overwhelming ambition of men to avenge some perceived wrongdoing. In addition to retaliation, there were other commonalities among vigilante groups to be sure. In her book *Lynchings in Kansas, 1850s–1932,* Harriet Frazier describes some of the salient features of mob justice. According to Dr. Frazier:

> *The mob never acts in self-defense and it never kills in order to prevent the imminent death of others. The general public perception is that a lynch mob always hanged its victim by the neck until dead. Often enough this occurred. However, the nature of the torment is not its essence; hanging, burning, shooting, dragging, drowning, a combination of these methods, or any other manner of causing intentional death that is utilized by a mob, qualify.... With one only known Kansas exception, mob members either remained unknown to coroner's juries; or if they were arrested, grand juries did not indict them, or if tried, trial juries did not convict them.*[137]

WARNING!
NOTICE IS GIVEN that any person found Pilfering, Stealing, Robbing, or committing any act of Lawless Violence will be summarily HANGED
Vigilance Committee.[138]

On January 29, 1861, Kansas was admitted to the Union, and Charles Robinson became the first governor of the state of Kansas. Taking office just two months before the outbreak of the Civil War, Robinson was preoccupied with wartime concerns. He also had to contend with accusations of the improper sales of bonds to fund the state militia. Robinson was acquitted of all charges, but only after resigning his position. This short tenure of Kansas's first governor provides some insight into the pervasive political unrest during the early years of statehood. Yet a more seditious problem loomed over Kansas: the continued violence between proslavery and free-state abolitionists, which now extended to the so-called Border Wars between Kansas Jayhawkers and Missouri Ruffians. As a result, forming vigilance committees became commonplace to protect communities against bands of outlaws taking advantage of the turmoil caused by war. Over the next several years, murderous raids would occur in both Kansas and Missouri, none bloodier than the massacre of residents in Lawrence, Kansas. Tragically, it was the collapse of a three-story, makeshift jail and the resulting deaths of four young female prisoners that played an important role in William Quantrill's decision to carry out a killing spree in Lawrence.[139]

On April 26, 1863, Brigadier General Thomas Ewing Jr. assumed command of the First Division of the Army of the Frontier. He was a thirty-three-year-old graduate of Brown University and the Cincinnati Law School who, in 1856, prior to the Civil War, moved to Leavenworth, Kansas, with his wife. He served as the first chief justice of the Kansas State Supreme Court and was known to be a free-state advocate. At the time, about five hundred U.S. Army Infantry troops were stationed along the border in parts of Kansas and Missouri north of the thirty-eighth parallel. Most of them were situated in Jackson, Cass or Bates County, Missouri, where rebel guerrillas were becoming more numerous. A telegram to the chief of staff at Fort Leavenworth, Kansas, on May 14, 1863, provides the following description of what was unfolding at the time:

> *They have all crossed the river from the north side, and are concentrating in the frontier counties between Kansas City and Fort Scott. Many are returning from the south, and their numbers are swelling daily. They are also making raids into the southwestern portion of Kansas, and a general state of alarm exists among the settlers, and as a last resort, for the protection of the loyal people of this State, which has furnished 30 per cent. More men than any other State to enter the service, I have been compelled to authorize the sheriffs of the border counties to raise a posse from among the few that remain at home for the protection of their laws and property. I shall furnish them such arms as I have directed them to cooperate with the regular forces. This is the only way that loyal people can be protected until I can have troops furnished me.*[140]

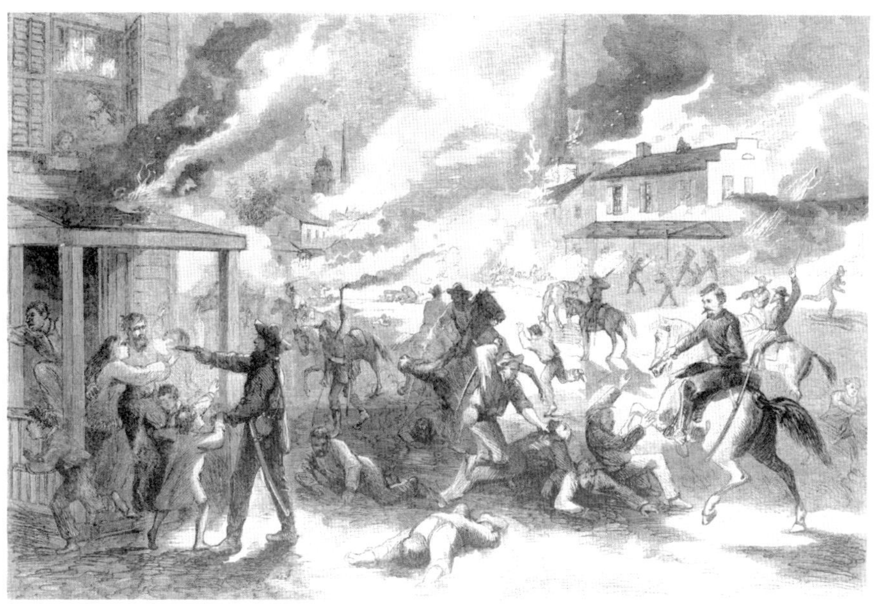

Drawing of the destruction of the city of Lawrence, Kansas, and the massacre of its inhabitants by the Rebel guerrillas, August 21, 1863. *Library of Congress.*

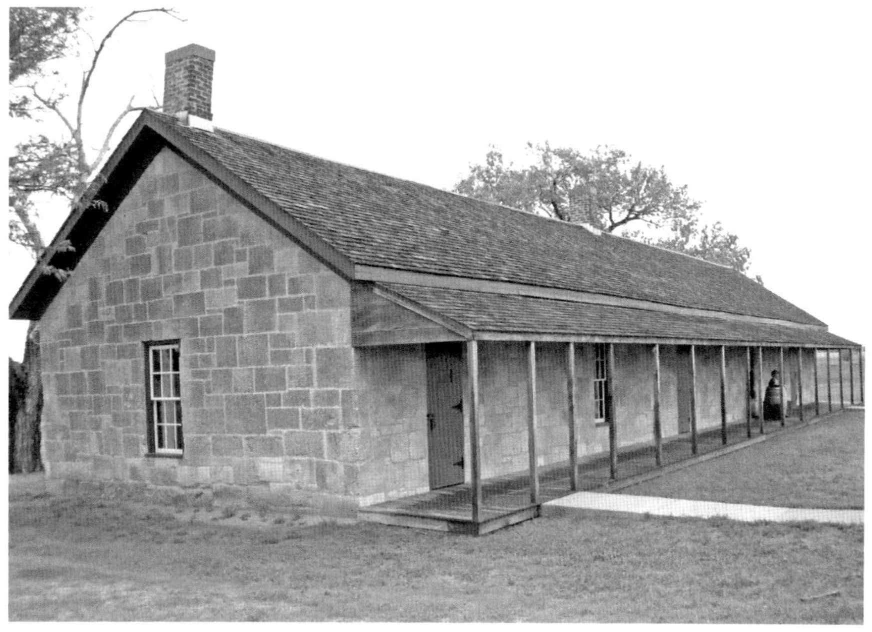

Military guardhouse at Fort Hays, Kansas. The guardhouse was the jail for soldiers who violated military rules or committed a crime in Hays City, which was less than a mile from the fort. Offenses ranged from disobeying an officer to murder.

Beginning in April 1863, Union troops began to arrest and detain many women in the Kansas City area who were said to be spying and gathering food and information for Missouri guerrilla commands and partisan rangers. The women were imprisoned in a three-story storefront building that had been converted into a jail. This makeshift jail suddenly collapsed on August 13, 1863, killing four women, including fourteen-year-old Josephine Anderson, sister of Bill Anderson, known as "Bloody Bill," who rode with

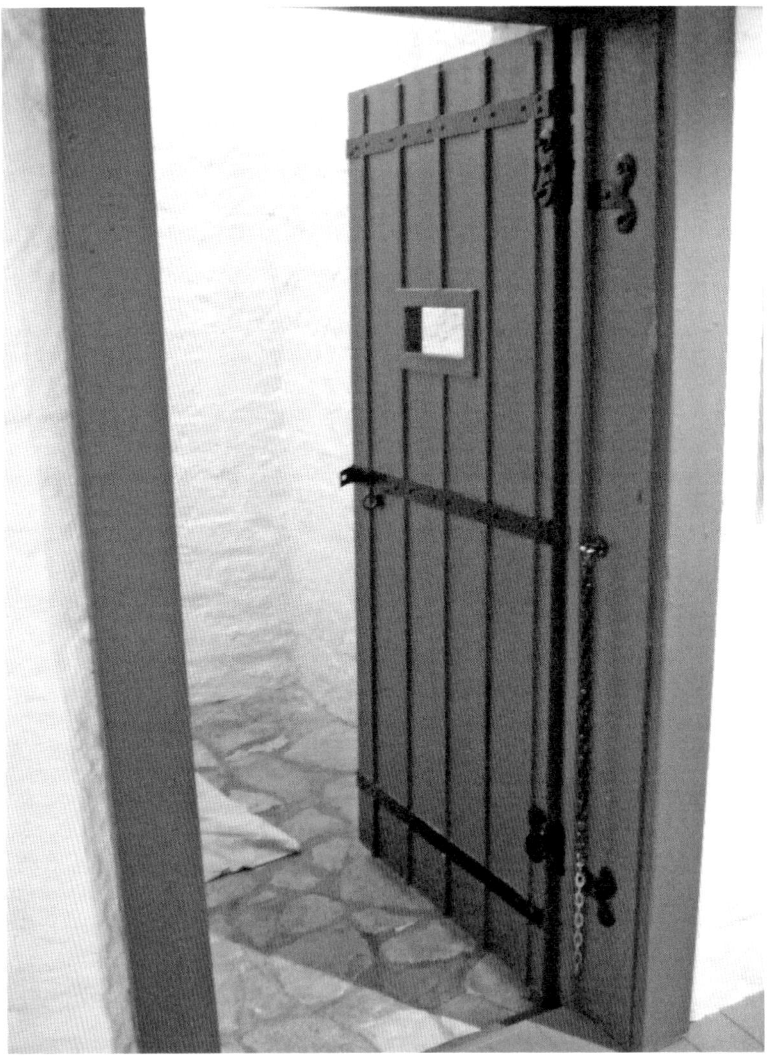

The Fort Hays guardhouse contained two jail cells, one seven by twenty-one feet and the other eleven by twenty-one feet.

Confederate guerrilla William Quantrill. Janie, the youngest of Anderson's teenage sisters, who had been shackled to a bed for unruly behavior, suffered broken legs, lacerations and a back injury.[141]

It has been suggested that the inner structures and supports of the building were actually damaged by guards, which caused the building to sink and eventually collapse.[142] Many historians believe this event was viewed as a deliberate act of murder committed by Union soldiers, and it played an important role in William Quantrill's decision to carry out the August 18, 1863 raid on Lawrence, Kansas. On that day, Quantrill's 450 guerrilla fighters entered Lawrence with a list of men to be killed and buildings to be torched to the ground. Quantrill had long wanted to raid the town for its role as the headquarters of the abolitionist movement that led to Kansas becoming a free state when it was admitted to the Union. His quest for revenge in Lawrence quickly turned into a massacre, with indiscriminate executions leaving between 140 and 200 men and boys dead. More than 180 buildings were set aflame during the butchery.

By the end of the Civil War, thousands of people had been displaced, most of whom were farmers and former slaves. Many took jobs in railroad construction, bringing them to the Great Plains. Accordingly, the population of Kansas grew, as towns were established along the routes of the transcontinental railroads. The stimulation of local building included courthouses, sheriff's residences and jails. In towns like Council Grove, Cottonwood Falls, Dodge City, Hays City, Topeka and Seneca, jails would be constructed to hold drunk soldiers, disorderly cowboys and outlaws. It was a time when legendary lawmen stood ready to step in and jail anyone who got out of hand. These lawmen required the building of permanent jails, like the iron jail of Lawrence, and could not rely on the guarded military encampments, provisional prison homes or modest jailhouses of the territorial period. Consequently, the makeshift jails of earlier times were replaced by limestone, brick and concrete structures with iron cells and elaborate locking systems. Jails would quickly become formal institutions across frontier Kansas during the second half of the nineteenth century.

Part IV
EXPANDING JAILS ACROSS THE KANSAS FRONTIER

There were thirty-three original counties organized by the territorial legislature in 1855, but it was not until after the Civil War that Kansas experienced a significant increase in population. Between 1865 and 1890, more than one million people would stream into Kansas seeking a new life on the frontier.[143] With the increased number of inhabitants came the formation of new townships and the need to build various types of public buildings, including jails. Traditional materials used to build jails depended, for the most part, on the abundance of materials readily available in the locale. Jailhouses of this period can be categorized into three types, including log construction, wood-frame construction and masonry construction, with three subtypes: concrete, stone and brick.

Construction of early jails was financed by local residents. Consequently, many were simple one-room buildings constructed directly on the ground with a dirt floor and no foundation. They were built entirely of hewn logs, each a foot square and notched at the ends, so that when laid in the wall, they mounted closely together. Occasionally, the jail was fitted with small iron gratings as windows. Many of these jails were in constant need of repair. Structures were extremely difficult to heat in the winter and scorching hot in the summer. In 1858, for example, the first jail in the county of Breckinridge (present-day Lyon County), Kansas, was at Americus, when that town was the county seat. This was a hewn-log structure, built less like a jail but more closely used as a "jail pen" to hold someone for a short time, perhaps overnight or during transit of a prisoner to another jail or the penitentiary.

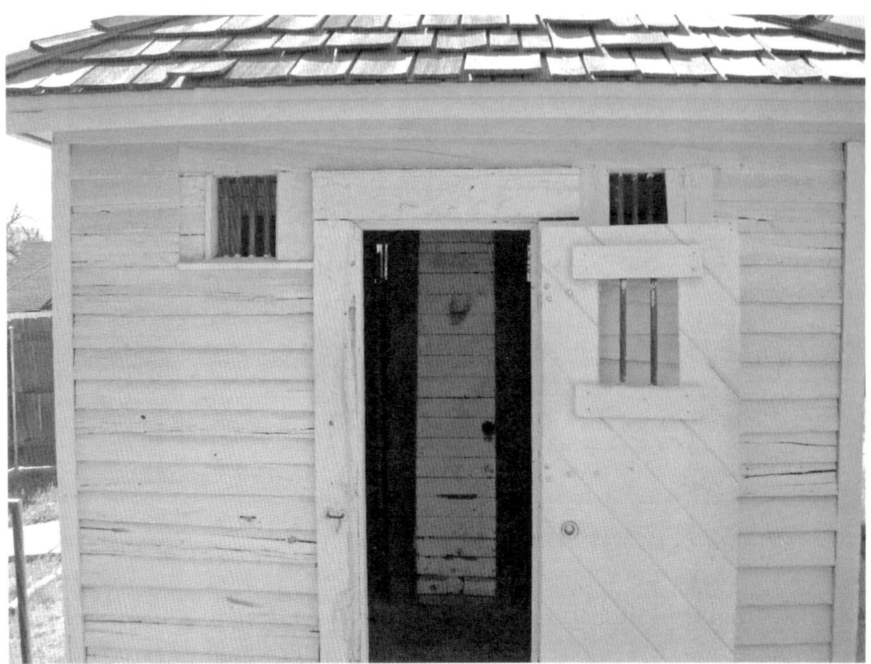

Front door entrance to the 1865 Fort Dodge, Kansas jail.

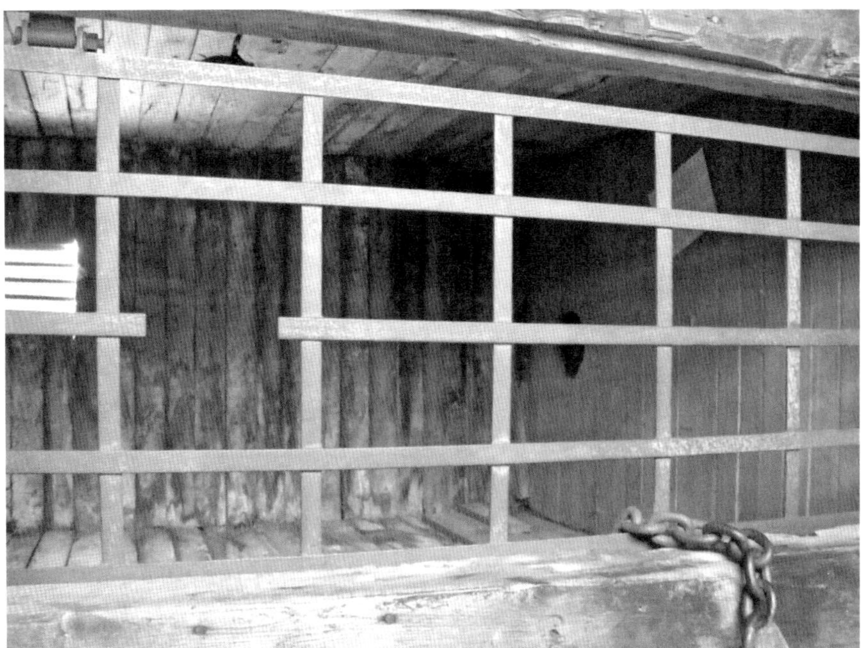

Iron cell door of the 1865 Fort Dodge, Kansas jail.

Another structure that symbolizes the crudeness of jail buildings during this period is the 1865 Fort Dodge, Kansas jail. It was a small, five- by eight-foot rough-hewn log structure, only six feet tall, and contained three cells to house prisoners at the fort until its closure in the 1870s. The only ventilation and source of light for the prisoners were the four small windows and the opening in the door. Prisoners generally slept on dirt floors, and there were no sanitary facilities. This calaboose was the U.S. Army's equivalent of a county jail and was mainly used to detain soldiers alleged to have committed crimes.

Building construction evolved rapidly in the eastern part of Kansas. Once sawmills began operations in the late 1850s, craftsmen built wood-framed jails out of oak, elm, sycamore, black walnut and several other types of trees. Most of the jails featured a strong entrance door, secured by heavy iron hardware, making it difficult to break down. Iron spikes were often used to strengthen walls and inhibit prisoners from sawing their way out. The old jail in Council Grove, Kansas, provides a good example of a wood-framed jail built in this period. The jail was originally constructed in 1870 as a two-story structure, with the jail on the ground floor and the sheriff's office above. Local historian and retired municipal judge Kenneth

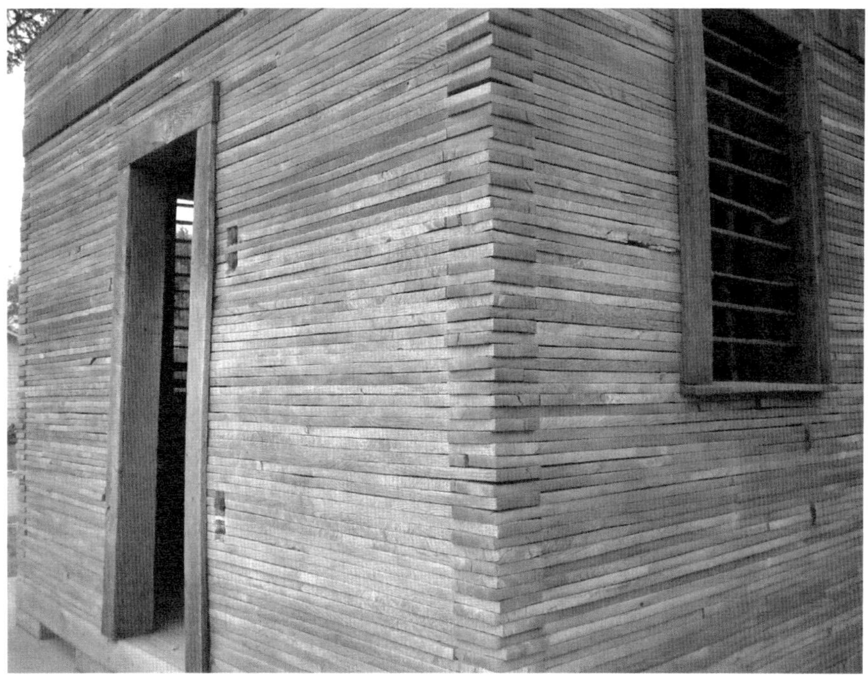

Front entrance of the 1870 jail in Council Grove, Kansas.

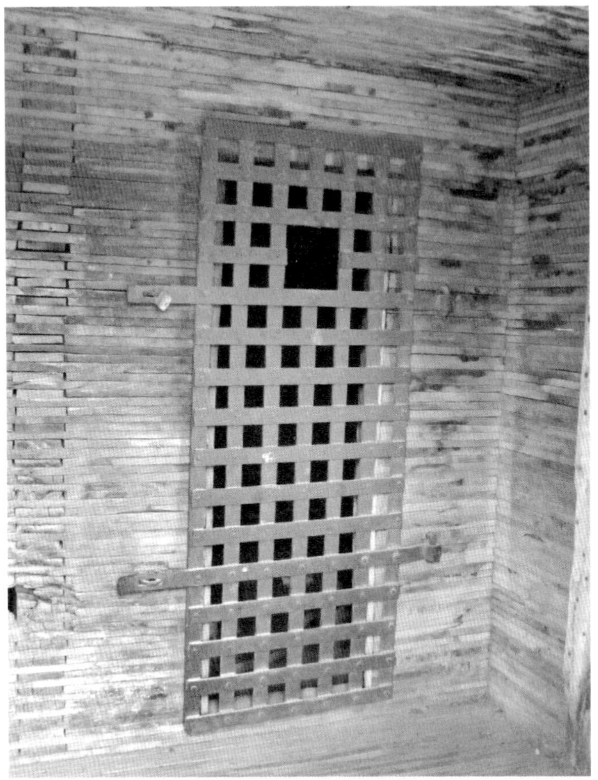

Jail cell of the 1870 jail in Council Grove, Kansas.

McClintock believes the jail was built at the south end of Washington Street, near Elm Creek, where there had previously been a log house. Like other towns growing in population, Council Grove needed a firm law enforcement presence and a fixed jail to securely keep those accused of crimes. Prior to the jail's construction, an incident occurred that reiterated that need. On February 2, 1867, just after midnight, a gang of disguised men in the frontier community of Council Grove, Kansas, took Jack McDowell from a log guardhouse and placed a rope around his neck. They promptly marched McDowell to a bridge over the Neosho River and hanged him for stealing horses. His body was left hanging there all night and in the morning as a warning to others. McDowell had ridden with Bloody Bill Anderson, Dick Yeager and other Missouri Partisan Rangers from William Quantrill's unit. It was of common opinion that, had McDowell not met his fate in Council Grove, it would have happened to him elsewhere before long.[144] Jack McDowell was the first known horse thief to be hanged in Kansas.[145]

10

FORTIFIED LOCKUPS

Jail construction quickly evolved from wooden buildings to hardened structures. The diminishing number of trees to the west throughout Kansas halted the advance of wooden jails, permitting only scattered and isolated occurrences of log and wooden jails in the western half of the state. Many of the wood-framed structures that were built succumbed to fire and were replaced with more permanent building materials. The presence of good-quality clay in the bottomlands for bricks and limestone deposits led to the development of large quarries and brickyards and determined the predominant building materials of many towns. Besides changing the type of materials to construct jails, architects began to vary their designs to address problems common to jails, such as making the building easier to maintain over its lifetime and designing structures that were more resistant to natural disasters.

Some of the most impressive surviving jail structures were constructed of stone and concrete masonry in the late 1800s. Like the wooden jails, these early jails often had only one room. A few featured oval roofs similar to the man-made caverns that were built by pioneers to function as root cellars and storm shelters but above ground. Iron stovepipes above the roof line suggest some of these jails had wood-burning capabilities—the only apparent concession to prisoner comfort.

Limestone was another popular building material for constructing jails. This sedimentary rock is hard enough to require a nail to scratch it and can be found throughout Kansas. In most cases, the rock for a jail could be

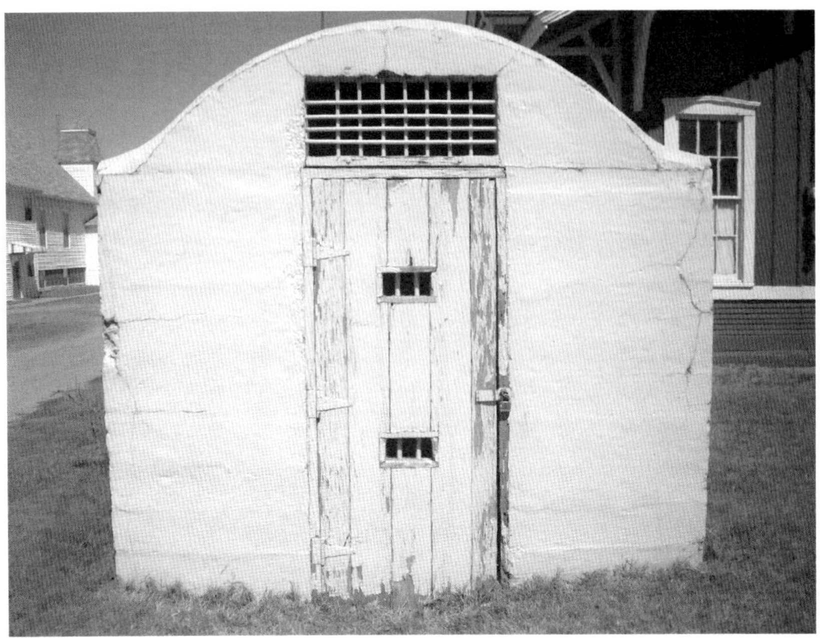

The 1890 city jail in Cunningham, Kansas. The building is made of concrete with a heavy, wooden entrance door.

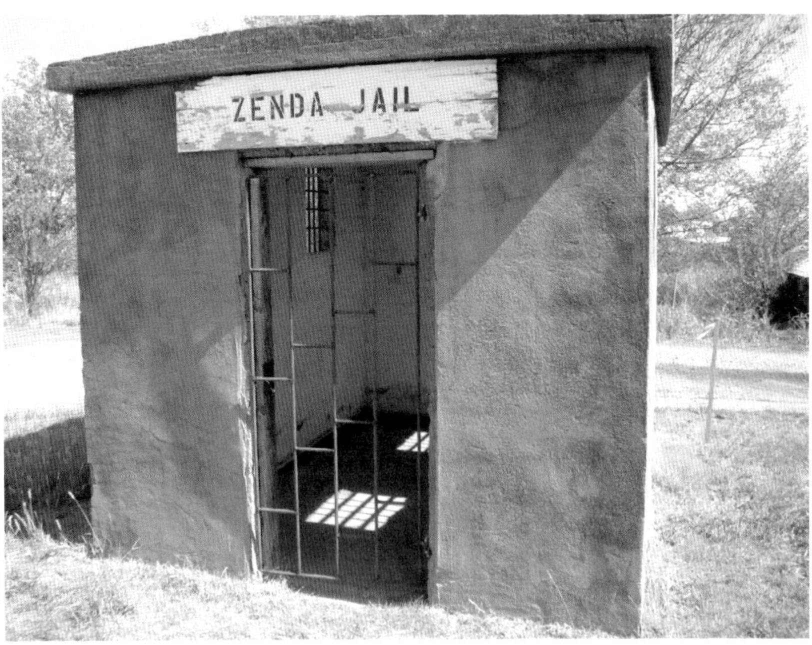

Front entrance of the 1887 city jail in Zenda, Kansas.

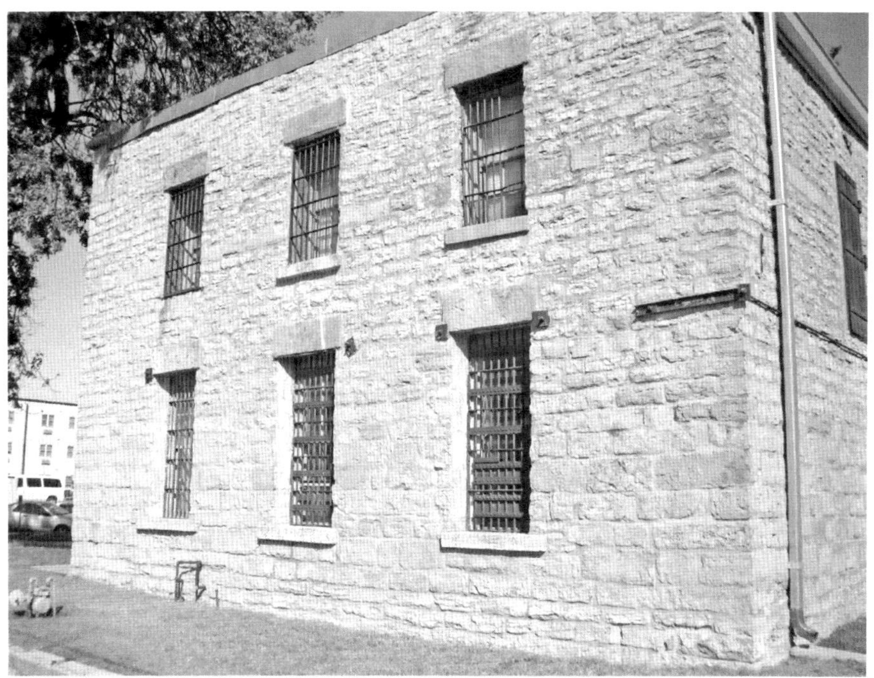

The 1869 Allen County (Iola), Kansas limestone jail. Prior to the jail being constructed, offenders were boarded at private houses at the cost of nine dollars per week.

quarried locally, and a local blacksmith fabricated the ironwork. Changing direction from the single-room structure, an example of a multiple-floor jail building is the Allen County Jail in Iola, Kansas, which was built in 1869 at a cost of $8,400. The jail was thirty feet across by thirty-seven feet deep, and the limestone walls exceeded two feet in thickness and housed prisoners in cells on both the first and second floors. Much of the floor on the lower level was made of Bandera marble, which is a type of flagstone rock found around Redfield, Kansas. From 1869 to 1891, the lower floor contained wooden cells, with an iron stairway to the second floor.[146] These cells were replaced in 1891 by a large steel cage manufactured in Covington, Kentucky, and brought to Iola for assembly. An article regarding the chrome steel cage appeared in the *Iola Register* on December 4, 1891, stating, "Even if the walls of the jail were torn down the prisoners could not escape."[147]

The Allen County Jail was the first jail in southeast Kansas and was in continuous use for eighty-nine years. Although described as being "strong enough to hold the strongest, slipperiest, and most expert of lawbreakers,"[148] this frontier jail had its problems with prisoner escapes. In July 1870, for

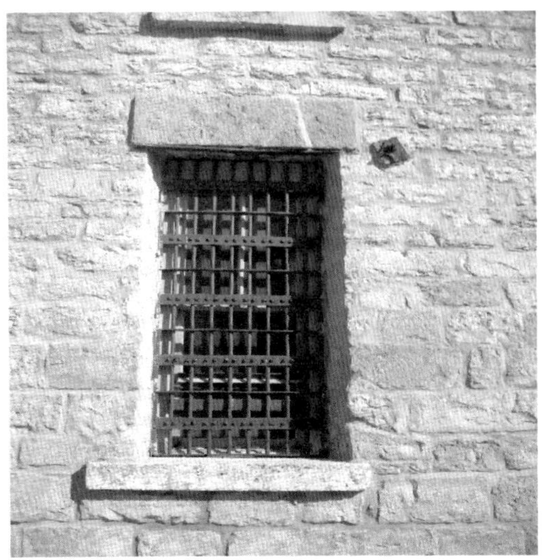

One of several heavy metal windows at the 1869 Allen County (Iola), Kansas jail.

example, six prisoners escaped by sawing off two bars of a window grate. The history of the jail is also marked with accounts of mob justice. One such event occurred on June 28, 1870, when an angry mob forcibly overpowered Sheriff John Harris and his deputy, John Walters, at the jail in Iola and grabbed Elzy G. Dolson, a Methodist minister from Humboldt, Kansas. Dolson had confessed to beating a young boy who was living with him, known to many as being his adopted son. The boy eventually died, and Dolson threw the body into an unused well, where it was discovered. The mob took Dolson to a barn two miles southwest of town, where he was hanged.[149]

Southeastern Kansas is known for hosting some of the state's most vicious murders during the late 1800s. For example, during the 1890s, Galena, Kansas, was a busy mining town. The seedy side of town offered many brothels and saloons to cater to the passing miners. At one house of prostitution, Nancy (Ma) Staffleback and six other relatives killed and robbed an estimated fifty clients. The killing spree was uncovered during the summer of 1897, when a stranger passing through town looked down a mine shaft at Pickers Point and saw a body, which was later identified as Frank Galbraith. Two of the Staffleback men (George and Ed) were charged with first-degree murder, and Ma Staffleback was charged with second-degree murder. All were convicted, and Ma Staffleback, who became known as "Galena's Bloody Madam," died in a Kansas prison in 1909.[150]

An even better depiction of murder in the southeastern part of Kansas was the serial killings by the notorious Bender family. In the 1870s, John Bender; his wife, Elvira; their son, John Jr.; and their daughter, Kate, conspired and killed at least eleven persons at their home, which doubled as a tavern and general store near the Osage Trail in Labette County, Kansas. This homestead became a place for weary travelers crossing the country to stop for a meal and sometimes take up lodging overnight. Feed was also provided for the travelers' horses. The

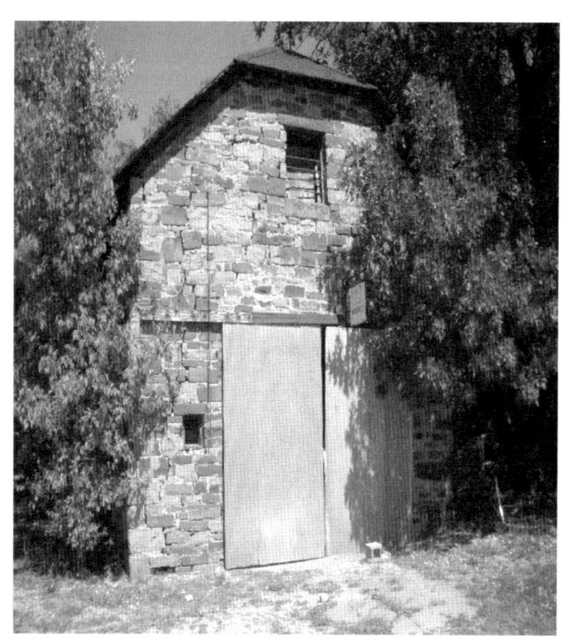

The 1888 native sandstone jail of Caney, Kansas.

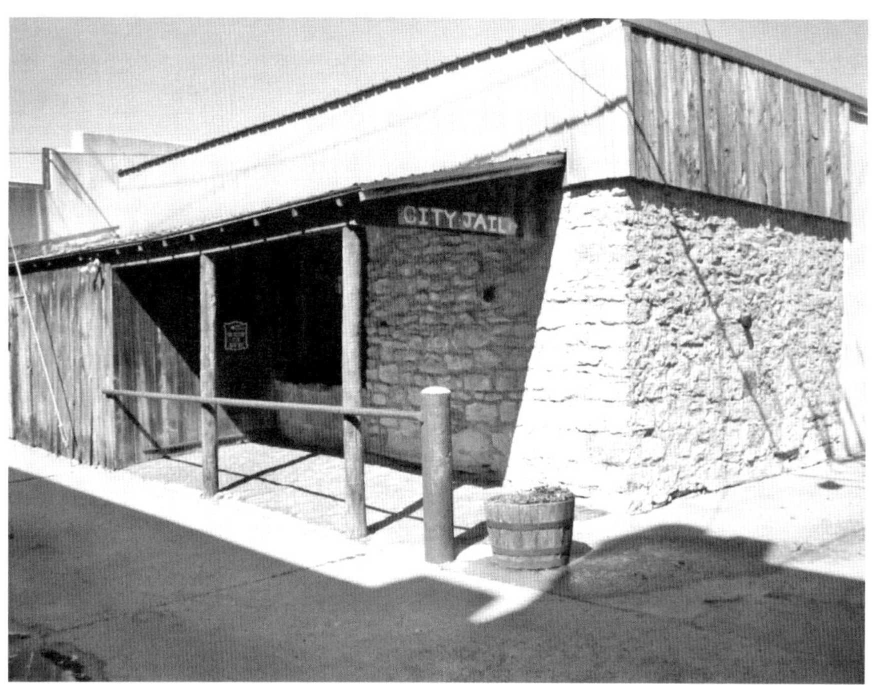

City jail in Coffeyville, Kansas. On October 5, 1892, Dalton gang members tied their horses outside the jailhouse while they robbed the C.M. Condon Bank and First National Bank.

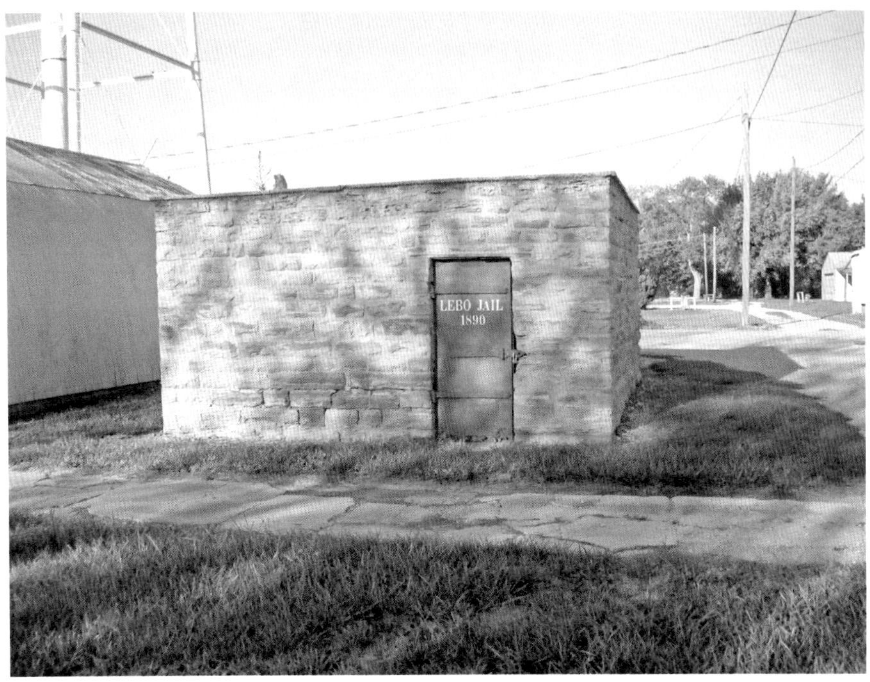

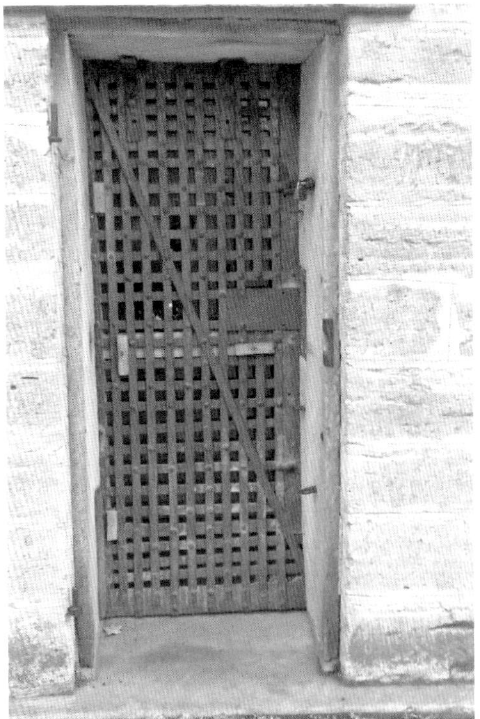

Above: The 1890 city jail of Lebo, Kansas.

Left: Iron lattice door entrance into the 1872 city jail of Louisville, Kansas.

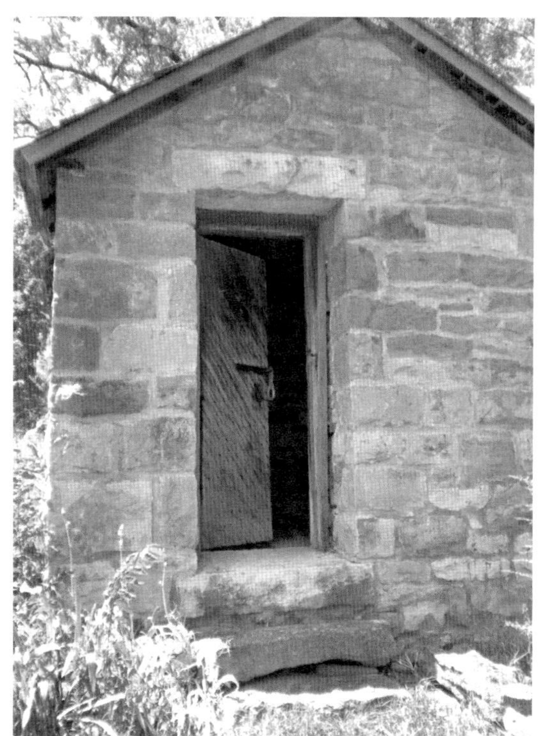

Right: The 1892 limestone jail in Lecompton, Kansas.

Below: Exterior view of the backside of the 1892 Lecompton, Kansas city jail.

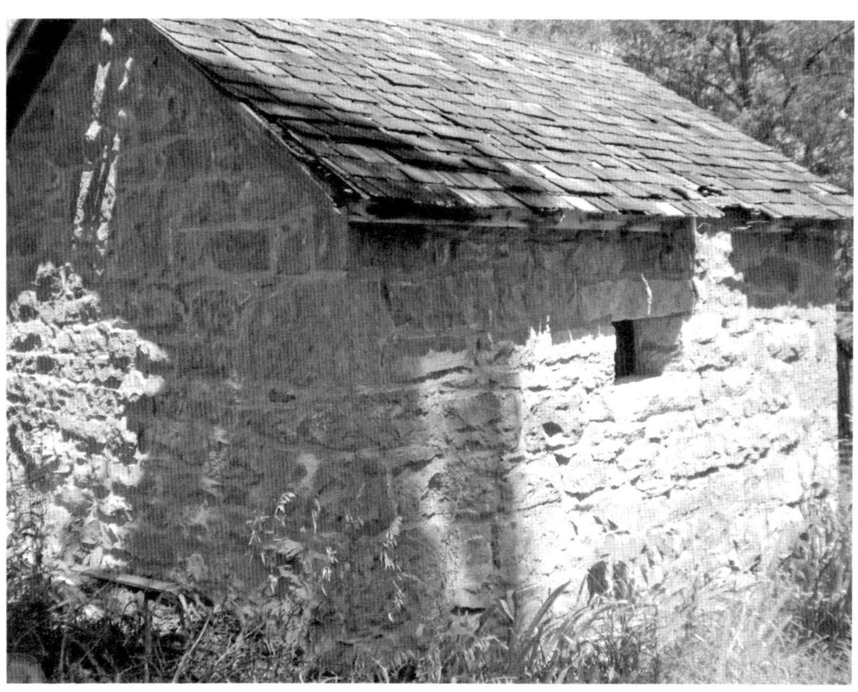

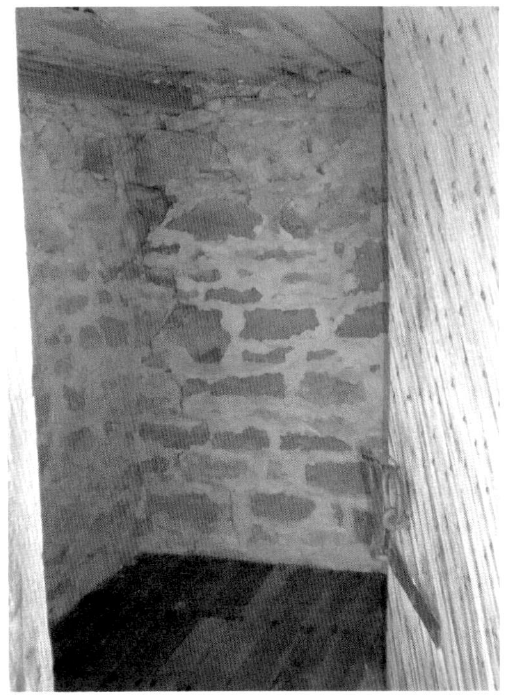

family's method of killing was a swift blow to the head of the victim from behind, followed by the slashing of the throat. The body was then dragged to a trapdoor that led to a cellar and dumped below until it could be buried somewhere on the prairie.

The killing spree would come to an end when Dr. William York visited the "Bloody Benders" when searching for a neighbor and his infant daughter who had traveled in the region during the previous winter but never returned. Dr. York would soon be reported missing, and in April, his brother, Colonel Ed York, came to Labette County leading a party of fifty citizens from Montgomery County. Arriving at the Bender home, Colonel York explained that his brother had disappeared, and he asked the family about whether they had seen him pass through the area. While admitting that Dr. York had stayed with them, the Benders

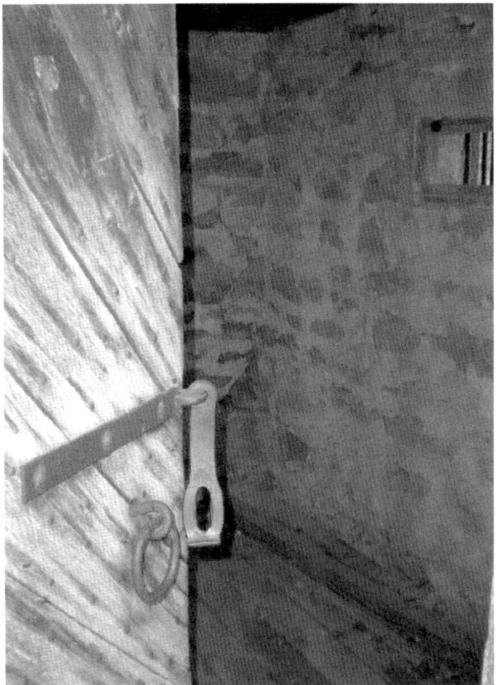

Top: Inside the city jail in Lecompton, Kansas.

Left: A view of the small dimensions inside the jail in Lecompton, Kansas.

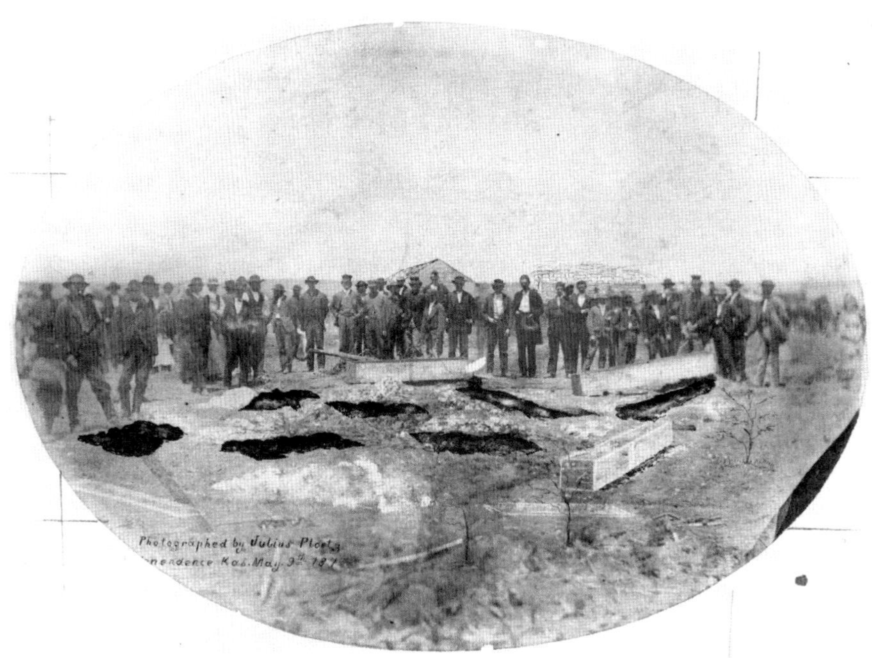

A photograph showing a large group of men looking at the graves of those murdered by the Bender family in Labette County, Kansas, May 9, 1873. *Kansas Historical Society.*

suggested the possibility that he had run into trouble with Indians. Colonel York agreed to the possibility but, a few days later, returned to the Bender property. He did not come alone, having convinced the sheriff to send deputies and local men from town. When they arrived, it became apparent that the Benders had abandoned the property. They found the cabin empty of food, clothing and personal possessions. A bad odor was noticed and traced to a trapdoor, nailed shut, underneath a bed. The men began searching the fields and the orchard around the house. Among the trees, they found eleven mounds of oddly shaped earth, and when the digging stopped, Dr. York's body was recovered, having been buried facedown with his feet barely below the surface. Many other bodies were allegedly found, but how many went undiscovered remains unknown.

Over the years, much of the focus on the murders committed by the Benders has been on Kate Bender. In 1880, a newspaper reporter from the *Chicago Times* wrote, "Kate was a red-faced, low-browed, square-shouldered amazon, strong enough to throw a bull by the tail, and everybody stood in awe of her. She made a pretense of practicing the healing art, and was known far and wide as a 'spiritualistic doctor.' Her cures were permanent, and her remedy was a hammer."[151] Although stories abound, the ultimate fate of the Bender family is uncertain.

Alongside its famously gruesome murders, another important marker of lawlessness identified with southeast Kansas was bootlegging. Sometimes referred to as the "Little Balkans," Cherokee, Crawford and Bourbon Counties became the geographical host to many small communities of emigrants from Albania, Bulgaria, Slovenia and other southeastern European countries. They came to the region in search of work in the coal mines. In 1874, Samuel Scammon and his three brothers from Illinois pioneered new methods of mining coal in southeastern Kansas, digging the first mine shaft in Cherokee County. Although many doubted that their room-and-pillar system would work in such shallow mines, this Cherokee County mine was soon producing forty carloads of coal a day.[152] Within a few years, underground mining became the principal method of coal mining in southeastern Kansas. The vastly increased demand for fuel, due to the enlarged railroad operations and the great increase in population, led to the rapid and extensive development of the coal region. By the early 1900s, one-third of the nation's coal was mined from southeast Kansas.[153]

On the occasion when a coal mine closed, some miners turned to making "mountain dew," despite an 1880 amendment to the state constitution that made the manufacture and sale of alcohol illegal. Though it may have started as a means of making an income to support hungry families, moonshining quickly turned into a booming criminal enterprise, as home brewing and distilling thrived in the late 1800s. Demand for the so-called hooch, fire water, elixir and hair of the dog increased during the Prohibition era of the 1920s and 1930s, as moonshine whiskey was consumed in speakeasies from New York to Chicago.[154] Enforcement of the law was hit or miss at best, as police often overlooked violations. On the rare occasion that an arrest was made, the average bootlegging conviction brought about a $100 fine and thirty-day jail sentence.[155] While jails across the country started to become overcrowded during the Prohibition era, the cause was not an increased jail population of bootleggers. On January 1, 1930, there were 116,670 prisoners in state prisons. Of these, only 4,037 (3 percent) were violators of the Prohibition laws. Of the 11,270 prisoners in federal penitentiaries, only 3,121 (27 percent) had been convicted on liquor charges.[156]

"Dram shop" is a legal term in the United States referring to a bar or tavern where alcoholic beverages are sold. Traditionally, it referred to a shop where spirits were sold by the dram, a small unit of liquid. In 1855, the Kansas Territorial Legislature enacted a law to regulate dram shops by

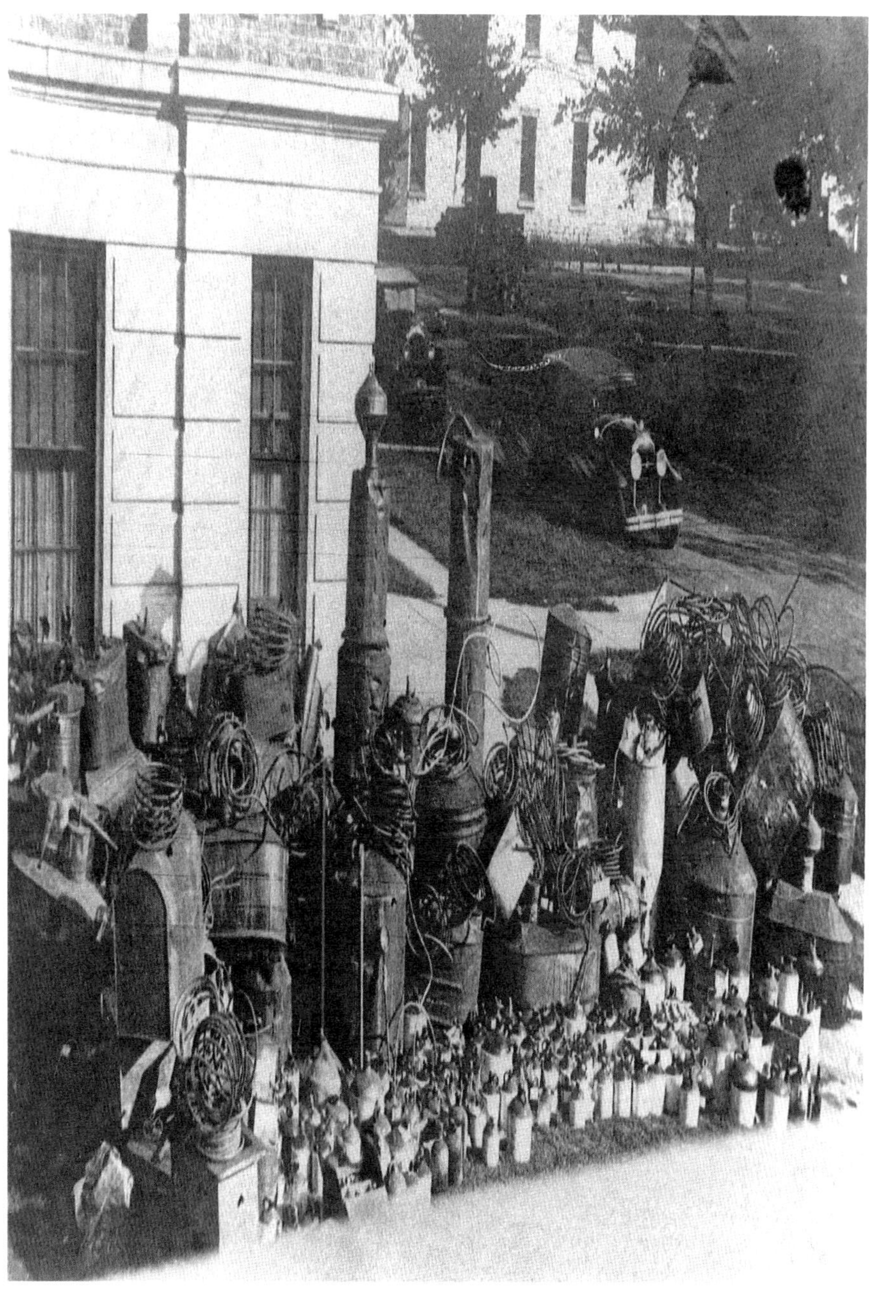

Moonshine stills confiscated in Crawford County, Kansas. *Courtesy of Kenneth Peak, PhD, University of Nevada–Reno.*

setting a license fee, which ranged from $100 to $300. An 1859 amendment to the law provided a civil cause of action against the seller, barterer or giver of intoxicating liquors if harm was caused "by any intoxicated person or in consequence of intoxication."[157] That law survived three challenges to its constitutionality and was included in the *General Statutes of 1868*.[158]

The Kansas dram shop law was extremely broad. Liability was not limited to vendors of alcohol, and physical injury to a third party was not required. The wide net cast by the statute was included in the 1881 revision when it stated:

> *Every wife, child, parent, guardian or employer, or other person who shall be injured in person or property, or means of support, by any intoxicated person, or in consequence of intoxication, habitual or otherwise, of any person, such wife, child, parent or guardian, employer or other person shall have a right of action, in his or her own name, against any person who shall, by selling, bartering or giving intoxicating liquors, have caused the intoxication of such person, for all damages actually sustained, as well as for exemplary damages; and a married woman shall have the right to bring suits, prosecute and control the same, and the amount recovered, the same as if unmarried; and all damages recovered by a minor under this act shall be paid either to such minor, or to his or her parents, guardian, or next friend, as the court shall direct; and all suits for damages under this act shall be by civil action in any of the courts of this state having jurisdiction thereof.*[159]

The broadness of the law is not surprising, as Kansas was long recognized as being in the forefront of the temperance movement.[160] Penalties for violation of the dram shop law included a $100 fine for selling without a license. A second or subsequent offense would be a fine of $100 and not less than five nor more than thirty days in the county jail. Selling to a slave without the consent of his master or selling liquor on Sunday resulted in the same penalties and forfeiture of the license.

The temperance movement in Kansas, spearheaded by the Woman's Christian Temperance Union, culminated with a prohibitory amendment to the Kansas constitution. Kansas was the first state to pass a prohibition law, yet sentiments of the citizens remained mixed and varied from county to county. Several counties were against a state prohibition on alcohol, including Wyandotte, Washington and Ford. In all, the November 1880 vote carried by a close margin of 92,302 for and 84,304 against.[161]

What soon followed were radical attacks on taverns throughout Kansas. Women rallied behind the banner of temperance, often engaging in direct protest. Prayer sessions inside saloons were common as testimony of their cause to purge the community of the evil that tempted men to consume spirits. If these methods failed, some women resorted to smashing the saloons to pieces with hatchets. The most famous of these reformers was Carrie Amelia Moore Nation. In 1889, Nation began her temperance work in Medicine Lodge, Kansas, by starting a local branch of the Woman's Christian Temperance Union. Her goal was to enforce the state ban on the sale of liquor, and she soon earned a reputation for being militant. Initially, she used rocks, bricks and other objects to damage property in saloons. She smashed her first saloon on June 1, 1900, in Kiowa, Kansas, and in December of the same year, she attacked a saloon in Wichita, Kansas, shattering a large mirror behind the bar and throwing rocks at a titillating painting of Cleopatra bathing. Nation then turned to smashing bar fixtures and stock with a hatchet. Her behavior provoked a tremendous uproar and sent her to jail repeatedly for disorderly conduct and disturbing the peace. She was jailed three times in Wichita, seven times in Topeka and many times in other places ranging from San Francisco, California, to Philadelphia, Pennsylvania.[162] Prohibition was adopted nationwide eight years later with ratification of the Eighteenth Amendment.

11

COWTOWN JAILS

The Pacific Railway Act of 1862 provided an estimated 180 million acres of land to railroad companies in exchange for building a transcontinental railroad across the country.[163] Soon, the Kansas Division of the Union Pacific Railway became a natural means of transportation in Kansas, stretching 675 miles, beginning at the Missouri River and extending westward to the Rocky Mountains. In its path were such towns as Abilene, Ellsworth and Hays City.[164] At the same time, the Atchison, Topeka & Santa Fe Railroad took advantage of funding to extend its rail service southwest through Kansas. By 1872, construction of the line had reached Newton, Great Bend and Dodge City.[165] Large stockyards quickly followed, attracting herds of cattle being driven northward from Texas. In the decade to follow, millions of steers and cows were moved along the Chisholm and Great Western Trails up to Kansas railheads. Once the vaqueros and cowboys had delivered their herds, they were ready to have a good time in the saloons and dance halls. Sometimes these trail hands got rowdy and violated town ordinances and state laws, which required them to be jailed.

The transcontinental railroad also brought other types of brazen characters, not afraid of hard work and hard living. An interesting description of these individuals is provided by Emerson Hough in his book *The Story of the Outlaw: A Study of the Western Desperado*:

> *They spent their wages as fast as they made it, hence, the gambler followed the rough settlements at the "heads of the rails." The murderer, the thief, the*

> *prostitute, the social outcast and the fleeing criminal went with the gamblers and the toughs. Those were the days when it was not polite to ask a man what his name had been back in the States. A very large percentage of this population was wild and lawless, and it impressed those who joined instead of being altered and improved by them. There were no wilder days in the West than those of the early railroad building. Such towns as Newton, Kansas, where eleven men were killed in one night; Fort Dodge, where armed encounters among cowboys and gamblers, deputies and desperadoes, were too frequent to attract attention; Caldwell, on the Indian border; hays City, Abilene, Ellsworth—any of a dozen cow camps, where the head of the rails caught the great northern cattle drives, furnished chapters lurid enough to take volumes in telling—indeed, perhaps, gave the stamp to the West which has been apparently so ineradicable.*[166]

In 1861, Abilene was designated as the county seat of Dickinson County, Kansas. Located on the north side of the Smoky Hill River in the Flint Hills region of the Great Plains, this small, sleepy community became the first of the great cattle towns of Kansas. In 1867, Abilene officials, aided by railroad executives, built stockyards for cattle herds coming up the Chisolm Trail from Texas. Soon, boardinghouses, hotels, brothels and saloons were built to accommodate the cowboys. Permanent residents of the town generally lived north of the railroad tracks to avoid Texas Street, an east–west thoroughfare that ran south of the railway. Texas Street was the location of establishments that catered to the cattle drovers and fostered a great deal of public disorder and vice.[167]

On May 2, 1870, city trustees drafted ordinances in an attempt to restore order. One such law prohibited loitering around brothels, gambling houses and saloons. When the law was enforced, the vagrant was levied a fine not to exceed $100 or jailed until the fine was paid.[168] Perhaps the most controversial regulation was an ordinance prohibiting the carrying of firearms within the city limits without a permit.[169] Local ordinances also created a police force and specified the duties of the city marshal and his deputies. The marshal, as "captain of the police, is to supervise the city jail, maintain a police record of all persons arrested and confined, together with their offenses and ultimate dispositions, and have charge of and control the entire police force of the town."[170]

Several attempts were made to hire a town marshal, but none of the men was capable of curbing the wildness of the cowboys. Town officials began to realize that it was going to take a man with grit to cope with the persistent foul play and lawlessness in town. On June 4, 1870, forty-year-old Thomas J. Smith was hired to keep the peace. He had previously served as a lawman in New York City; Bear, Wyoming; and Kit Carson, Colorado. In describing the new lawman, Mayor Theodore Henry wrote:

> *Tom Smith was a fine looking, broad shouldered, athletic man about five feet eleven inches in height, who tipped the scales at 170 pounds, stood erect, had grayish blue eyes, auburn hair and light mustache. He was gentle in manners, low-toned in speech, deferential in the presence of official superiors, and brave beyond question. He deserves first place in the gallery of frontier marshals.*[171]

Marshal Smith and his deputy operated the first jailhouse in Abilene, a sixteen- by sixteen-foot building located in the heart of Texas Street next to the G.B. Seely mercantile store. The jail was constructed of two- by six-inch wooden planks nailed together.[172] This type of structure, common between 1870 and 1910 to construct dwellings, was known as a plank house, box house or battened box house. It's likely that the jail walls were built entirely of the boards with planks extending from the foundation to the roof. The low cost for materials and small amount of required carpentry skills made it a popular construction type in communities where a quick and inexpensive jail was in demand. Beside Abilene, plank jails were constructed in other Kansas towns, such as Wichita, Burlingame and Wyandotte.[173]

At one time during an early phase of its construction, a band of raucous cowboys demolished the partially built jail. It was soon reassembled, and the jail was eventually completed and ready for use, this time under armed guard.[174] The town also built a brick and stone courthouse, the first structure of any material other than wood.[175]

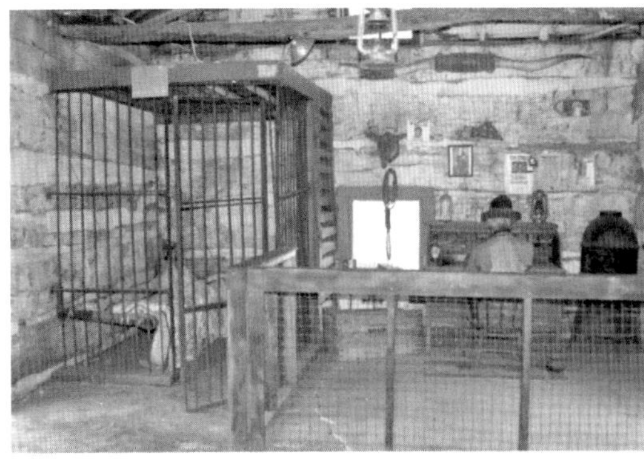

Old Town jail in Abilene, Kansas.

Tragically, Marshal Smith was killed in the line of duty only four months after taking office. While assisting in the arrest of suspected killer Andrew McConnell at a dugout outside town, Smith was shot in the chest. Although he was mortally wounded, the Abilene marshal returned fire, wounding McConnell. A second assailant by the name of Moses Miles struck Smith in the head, rendering him unconscious. Miles then seized an axe and attacked Smith, nearly severing the lawman's head. McConnell and Miles fled and remained wanted men for the first-degree murder of Smith. It took nearly two years before the two fugitives were captured, and they were both convicted and sentenced to life in prison.[176]

The next man to wear the city marshal badge in Abilene was Bill Hickok. You'll recall Hickok had served as constable in Monticello, Kansas. By the time of his arrival in April 1871, Hickok had added U.S. deputy marshal at Fort Riley, Kansas; U.S. deputy marshal and special policeman at Hays City, Kansas; and sheriff of Ellis County, Kansas, to his lawman résumé. He was well known to the people of Abilene, having been prominently featured in the Kansas press. Hickok would serve as the voice of law and order in this cowtown until December 1871.[177]

In August 1887, construction of a new Dickinson County jail began in Abilene. A.H. Paul and R.B. Jacobs, Contractors, won the bid to build both a high-security jail and a jailer's residence. The ironwork was provided by P.J. Pauly Iron Works.[178] It took seven months for the project to be completed, and when opened in May 1888, the jail was considered "a model structure for the purpose intended." An article written for the *Abilene Reflector* newspaper described the jail:

> *To give an adequate description of this building, which is an ornament alike to the city and county, is difficult. It reflects great credit upon the various firms interested in its construction. The lower floor is fitted up with nine cells, a sheriff's residence of five rooms and jailer's office. On the second floor are three cells for females, a cell for the sick and a half dozen rooms of the sheriff's residence. Six more cells can be placed on this floor and as many in the basement, if necessary. Throughout the entire building are water pipes, numerous ventilation flues and every arrangement that can add convenience and healthfulness to the building. The woodwork is elegantly finished in natural colors and is a proof of what John Lancaster can do in that line. Mr. Kummerland has the cornice work in the most admirable state of perfection, while John Hill deserves praise for the excellent system of plumbing put in. The Pauley Jail Company which manufactured and*

> *placed the steel work have given the county a lasting piece of workmanship. Messrs. Paul & Jacobs, the contractors, have added much to their already good name as reliable builders.*
>
> *Altogether the structure is a model and we do not see how C.B. Hopkins, the architect, could have planned a more convenient or handsomer one.*
>
> *The cost has been about $13,000.*[179]

Locals in the Abilene community had become increasingly weary of the lawlessness. In response, Abilene officials amplified the number of city ordinances in an attempt to restrain the undesirable behavior of the cowboys. At the same time, numerous Abilene ranchers became outraged when splenic fever from the Texas Longhorns began killing their domestic livestock. Hostility toward the cattle drovers started to outweigh the economic benefits of having them in town. Consequently, cattle herds were rerouted a bit west and farther down the track.

By July 1871, a significant portion of the Texas cattle drives had pushed sixty miles southwest to newly built stockyards in the city of Ellsworth, the county seat of Ellsworth County, Kansas. Between 1871 and 1875, Ellsworth was a main terminus of the Texas cattle trade in Kansas, shipping two hundred cars of cattle per day. By 1873, some 150,000 head of cattle were shipped from Ellsworth, and catering to the cattle industry netted the townspeople their expected profit. But so, too, did a full assortment of trouble from the gamblers, prostitutes and other seedy characters. Predictably, the town's saloons and gambling houses would operate day and night, every day.

While violence was commonplace, Ellsworth could boast of one advantage over Abilene: a police force, a courthouse and a jail. The county jail was built by the Kinear and Kendall Construction Company in 1873 on Court Street, immediately behind the courthouse, which had been built the previous year. It was a two-story limestone jail, thirty-six feet wide by fifty feet long. The upper story was a residence for the sheriff and his family and accommodated a few county offices, including a courtroom. The lower story was partitioned off into jail cells. Windows in the jail section were six feet from the ground, sixteen inches wide by twenty-three inches high. The depth of each of the windows was thirty inches with bars. The total cost of the jail and sheriff's residence was $4,600, and it took about one year to construct the building. It was said that the new jail was the most comfortable place in town but that not too many should crowd into the place at once.

The jail was plagued by escapes, including the very first prisoner. John M. Gruder had been arrested and charged with grand larceny. Gruder

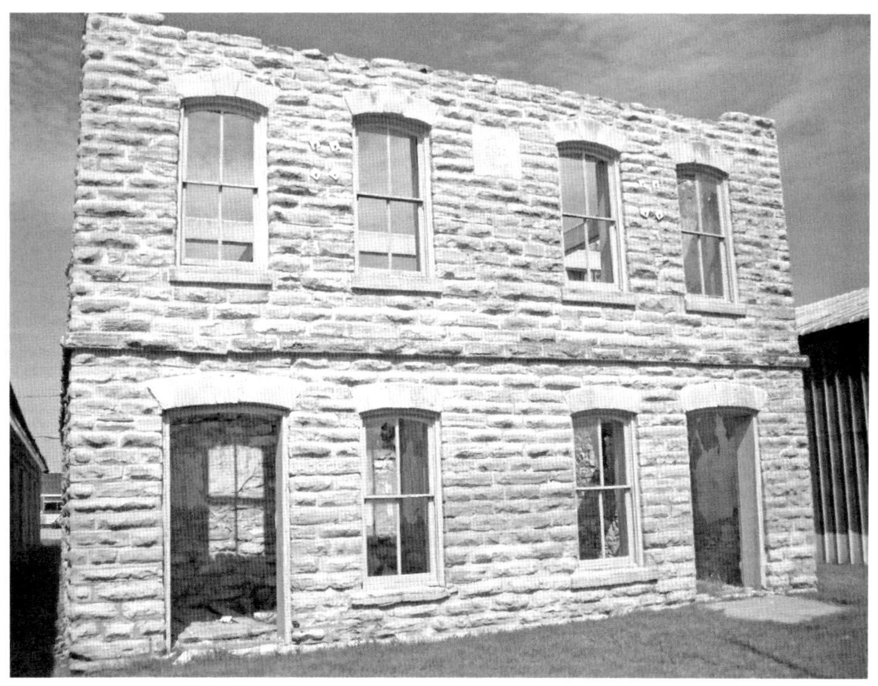

Front entrance of the 1873 Ellsworth County Jail.

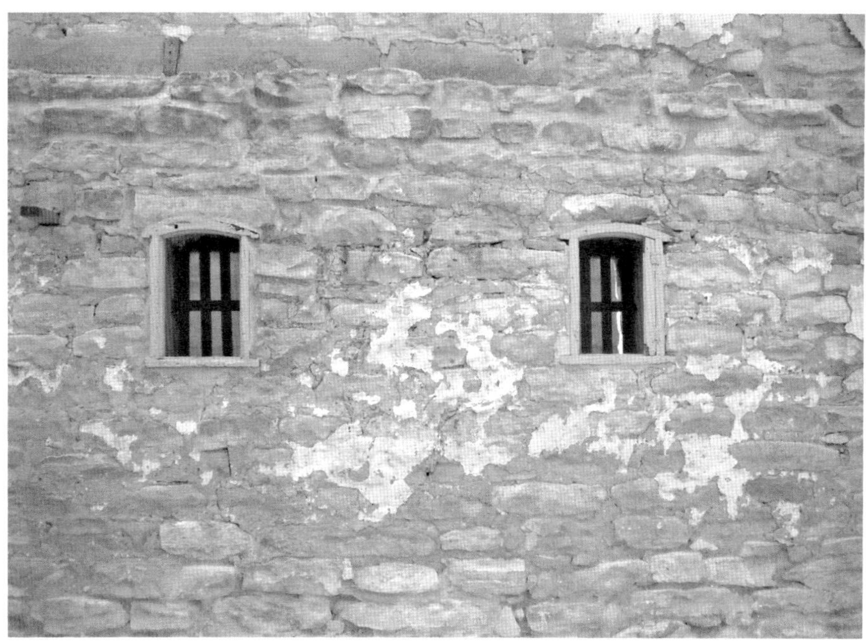

Last remaining side wall of the Ellsworth County Jail with barred windows.

was locked up in the Ellsworth County Jail but escaped a mere eight days later. The *Ellsworth Reporter* announced, "The sheriff is not at all to blame as the building is not fully ready for prisoners." It was said that Gruder escaped because the jail had yet to install all the locks.[180] Many other jail escapes would happen in Ellsworth over the years. In 1882, Lorenzo Dow Beal, known to be the "great western cattle thief," and three others escaped the jail.[181] Beal would be arrested, returned to jail and sentenced in Ellsworth District Court to twelve years hard labor in the penitentiary.[182] In 1897, two burglars by the names of Isham Douglas and Charles Brody escaped by sawing through the cell bars. It was later discovered that the men were part of an outlaw gang that assisted their escape. A reward of fifty dollars was offered for their recapture.[183] In the early 1900s, George Park (aka George Hensley) escaped from jail after being arrested for burglary in Ellsworth. He would be shot and killed while fleeing from a store burglary in Perry, Oklahoma.[184]

While the old limestone building served its purpose for the next three decades, a new county jail was eventually constructed in 1911. This was a large, two-story rectangular building with red-brick exterior walls and native stone foundation, again constructed as both a jail and sheriff's residence. A gable roof extended from the front hip to form a full-height front porch, supported by two-story, round Ionic wood columns. The building became a prominent structure in downtown Ellsworth.[185]

Ellsworth's days as a thriving cattle hub came to an end by 1875. The Texas cattle drives moved to other locations in Kansas, as the railroads pushed into south-central and southwestern portions of the state. At the same time, the Kansas legislature passed and revised quarantine laws regulating the number of Texas longhorns entering the state. These laws aimed to diminish the effect of splenic fever, a deadly bovine disease carried by infected longhorns and contagious to local livestock. Quarantine lines were altered several times, shifting the cattle drives farther south and westward, eliminating Ellsworth from the cattle trade. Longhorns would jam stockyards in Caldwell and Dodge City during the remainder of the 1870s through the mid-1880s. Although Ellsworth's shipping pens were now empty, the town had gained the reputation as a wild and wicked place. The anecdote became "Abilene the first, Dodge City the last, but Ellsworth the wickedest."

Texas cattle herds headed for Dodge City, a shipping point on the Santa Fe Railroad line. Thousands of cattle passed through the town's stockyards, and Dodge City's population swelled overnight. Like other cowtowns, Dodge City featured the usual assortment of saloons, gambling halls and brothels that catered to buffalo hunters, gamblers, soldiers, railroaders and gunfighters. With the addition of rambunctious cowboys, Dodge City became "Queen of the Cowtowns."

Mixing whiskey, women and cards was a natural formula for disorderly conduct. In the early years, arrest for drunkenness meant being thrown into the town's "cooler," which was simply an old well about fifteen feet deep. According to one newspaper account, "The first calaboose in Dodge City was a well dug down to the first water, in which police cases were placed, with feet tied. The men were pulled out by a rope. When more than two men were put in the same hole, fighting was the result."[186] The first actual jail building was constructed on South Front Street in 1875. It was a modest two-story wooden structure, with the jail occupying the ground floor and the top floor accommodating city offices and the police court administered by police judge Daniel Frost. The wood jail operated until 1876, then moved to a newly constructed courthouse and jail building, which cost $8,000.[187] Prior to its completion, Ford County prisoners were housed in jails in Shawnee and Reno Counties. The jail occupied the basement of this limestone and brick county building and was quickly nicknamed the "lime kiln."[188] The keepers of the new jail were also the first official lawmen in Dodge City and included Ford County sheriff Charles Bassett, Dodge City marshal Larry

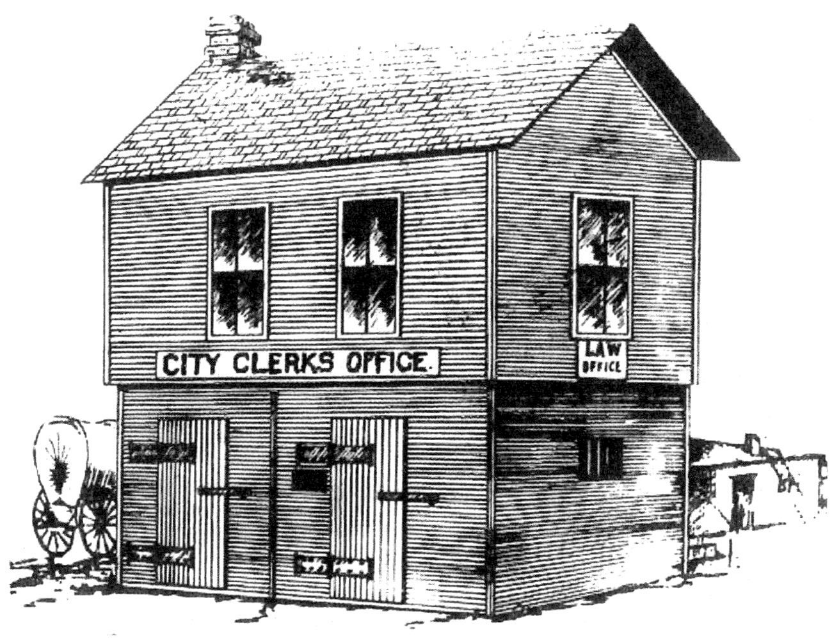

Drawing of the 1875 Dodge City Jail. *Boot Hill Museum, Dodge City, Kansas.*

Deger and city deputy marshal Wyatt Earp.[189] Bassett served two terms as sheriff and eventually became the town's city marshal. Deger became the mayor of Dodge City. Earp served as deputy marshal from 1876 to 1877 and 1878 to 1879.

"Hoosegow," "gray bar hotel" and "pokey" are just a few monikers for jail. As noted, in Dodge City, the jail was often referred to as the "lime kiln" by the locals (especially prisoners who frequented the lockup) and in newspaper reports—a fitting metaphor considering a lime kiln is a heap with walls built around it to confine wood or coal that, when heated, converted limestone into lime. Here are a couple excerpts from the *Dodge City Times* in which "lime kiln" was used to symbolize the jail in Dodge City:

> *Two worthy birds, "Stock Yards Shorty" and a cowboy, participating in a little slugology yesterday morning, in front of Jake Collar's store. After exchanging a few slugs, Shorty knocked the cow boy through one of Mr. Collar's large window lights. The cow boy in return drew a crimson stream from Shorty's proboscis. Our worthy Marshal interfered in their innocent amusement, and took them off to the lime kiln.*[190]
>
> *Frank Edwards spent a short respite in the lime kiln this week, until some of his "friends" obtained a key from the marshal and let him out. This surprised our hero, and struck him as not being good law. When his trial came up he appeared before the terrible Judge, and brushing the lime from his after-deck as he spoke, said: "There's something wrong Judge, if I was legally drunk, what was I unlegally* [sic] *let out for?" With this the case went to the court who said no complaint had been made and it was therefore not a legal drunk.*[191]

Most public order violations required the wrongdoer to pay a fine rather than to be locked up in the jail. In 1883, for example, the mayor and city council passed a city ordinance titled "An Ordinance for the Suppressing of Vice and Immorality within the City of Dodge City."[192] The law required that any person found to be operating a brothel could be fined between $10 and $100. Soon, other ordinances followed, prohibiting vagrancy, alcohol, gambling, use of opium and dance halls. These expanded regulations were often ignored, and violators found themselves locked up in jail.[193] Questions about the security and sanitary condition of the jail ensued, causing the local newspaper to publish the following observation in 1884:

> *Ford County needs a new jail. The prisoners confined in the present dungeon are suffering. An addition ought to be erected to the court house building, and*

> *the building thus made secure, affording more office facilities, and a new jail made of the basement.*[194]

There were escapes, like the one involving seven prisoners who absconded by digging under the building foundation with a case knife and chisel. It took them three weeks to execute their escape, according to another prisoner, who, at the time of the escape, was in town on a shopping trip with a deputy sheriff.[195] One of the more amusing escapes occurred some years later, when it was reported:

> *Of the five men who broke jail at Dodge City recently, one of them returned the next morning and gave himself up. He said he had walked all night and just after daylight while walking along the road saw a sign which said 2½ miles to Dodge City. He said he thought if that was the best he could do after an all night walk, he might as well be in jail. So he returned and gave himself up.*[196]

Dodge City held the cattle trade for ten years, the longest of any cowtown. In 1885 though, the Kansas legislature revised quarantine laws that would signal the end of the state's role in the Texas cattle industry.[197] Texas cattle herds were barred from entering Kansas between March and December, triggering a smaller number of herds driven into Kansas the following year. The one exception was found in Caldwell, Kansas, a small town so near the Oklahoma border that it was able to openly accept Texas cattle, albeit within the state's quarantine region. Caldwell became known as the the "Border Queen" town and, in its short history as a cowtown, rivaled Dodge City in the number of homicides of lawmen, cowboys and gamblers.[198] In 1884, a two-story city hall was built that housed a women's jail on the top floor. The city's fire wagons and men's jail were housed on the ground floor. In time, the railways would be extended into Texas, eliminating the need for cattle herds to be pushed up the trails north to the frontier towns of Kansas. The era of the Wild West frontier cowtown had come to an end, and so, too, did the simultaneous departure of prostitutes, gamblers and rowdy cowboys.

12

THE SQUIRREL CAGE OF WICHITA

For a few years, starting in the early 1870s, Wichita shared the distinction of being a cattle town. Town officials understood that gambling, whiskey and prostitution were essential services if the cattle trade was to be kept. They also recognized that keeping the vices in check meant Wichita needed a jail for lawmen to hold prisoners. Initially, prisoners were held in storefronts not suited to hold them. An excerpt from the November 24, 1870 edition of the first newspaper in the area, the *Wichita Vidette*, sums up the situation:

> *We have seen printing offices used for almost everything, but never knew of one being used for a jail until last night. On said night our office was made a place for the safe keeping of three prisoners. As the county is too poor to build a jail, and we are wealthy, we shall not present a bill for jail fees.*[199]

Thereafter, an old vacant building served as a makeshift calaboose. However, in April 1871, a committee was formed to study a site location and decide how a jail could be financed by the city. A few months later, a sixteen- by eighteen-foot wooden structure was built from Kansas cottonwoods. Countless escapes over the next couple years prompted county commissioners to request taxpayer approval for $10,000 to construct a new Sedgwick County Jail. The referendum passed, and the county quickly moved to accept bids for a jail that included three steel-clad cells. One newspaper in 1874 noted, "Work is rapidly progressing on the Wichita jail. We don't know of any place where a good jail is needed more."[200] By November, Wichita had a new jail with iron cells manufactured by a foundry in Atchison, Kansas. Security was still a big problem, and escapes still occurred routinely. In 1875, for example, ten prisoners escaped from the jail by cutting out a portion of a brick wall with a knife.[201] One of the more publicized escapes occurred in May 1884, when Peter Culpepper, a man in his mid-twenties, was charged with murder and locked up at the Sedgwick County Jail on $5,000 bail. On January 22, 1885, Culpepper walked out of the jail, along with three other prisoners. They had been aided in their escape, and according to a newspaper account, "There was no crookedness so far as the sheriff and his attendants were concerned. A crippled prisoner who had been allowed to occupy the corridors outside of the cages made a key of babbit [*sic*] metal and let the desperadoes out."[202]

Wichita suffered from the stigma of keeping jails that were anything but secure. The town wasn't alone, though, as jailbreaks occurred in every cowtown. In truth, jails weren't then, and are still not today, escape-proof when prisoners are left unattended. In the frontier era, the keepers of the jail were primarily the law officers. But city marshals and the county sheriffs were counted on foremost to uphold the law. Attending to the affairs of the cowboys often set a precedence that keeping the peace in town came first and watching the jail prisoners second.

Keepers of the Jail: The Local Lawmen

Sheriff	A sheriff is a county official elected by the public.
	An undersheriff is appointed by the sheriff. One person holds this position.
	A deputy sheriff is appointed by the sheriff. Several people may hold this position.
	A township constable is an elected position of the townships of the county.
City Marshal	A city marshal is appointed by the mayor.
	An assistant marshal is appointed by the marshal. One person holds this position.
	A policeman is appointed by the marshal. Several people may hold this position.
	A special policeman is appointed by the marshal when circumstances warrant.

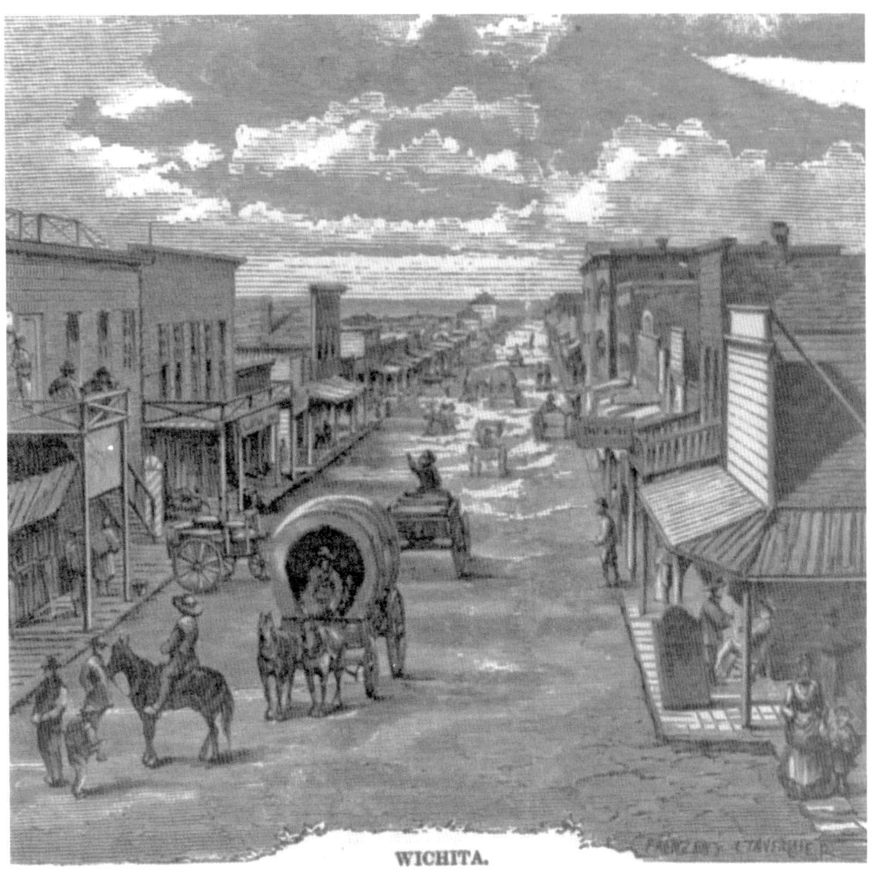

WICHITA.

In January 1888, citizens voted in support of a proposed $200,000 bond measure to build a new Sedgwick County Courthouse and Jail to be located in Wichita. The plan called for the jail to be constructed first, and when completed, the new courthouse would follow. A few months later, a contract was awarded to Pauly Jail Building and Iron Works to construct a jail, sheriff's office and residence at a cost of $47,250. The company received the contract to provide the iron and steel work, but all other branches of the work were subcontracted to city contractors and laborers. As far as the members of the grand jury who inspected the old jail were concerned, the letting of a contract to build a new jail couldn't have come soon enough. Their report, filed with the county commissioners, provides a glimpse into the conditions at the old jail:

> *We, the grand jury in and for Sedgwick county, in the state of Kansas, sitting at the May term of the district court in and for said county and*

> *state, charged by said court as a grand jury to inspect the county jail of said county and to determine for ourselves what, if anything, is needed for the safety, convenience and proper repairs of the same, and to submit to the board of county commissioners by report such examination and result of the same, do hereby report that we have made such examination and inspection, and do hereby report the following facts and recommendations: We find that forty-one men and five boys are now confined in the county jail in cells intended to accommodate twenty four persons. Some of the prisoners seem to be less than 12 years of age, and their baby eyes peer through the same iron grates of miserable pens poorly ventilated, called for the want of a better name, "cells," with full grown men. Some of the men are held by the United States authorities charged with murder and other heinous offenses committed in the territory. It is the deliberate judgment of this jury that the present condition of affairs at the jail is a disgrace to the people of Sedgwick county. The jail is overcrowded; it is poorly ventilated and in the basement is a pool of stagnant water that we consider endangers not only the health of the prisoners, but of the sheriff and his assistants who are compelled to reside in the building.*[203]

The architectural design of the new jail and sheriff's office and residence was unique for its time. The structure was large (seventy-five feet by ninety-three feet), having two full stories, a basement and an attic. The foundation and exterior were constructed of stone and brick, and entrances were kept separate—one to the sheriff's residence and another to allow public access to the sheriff's office and jail. The residence contained a vestibule, parlor, dining room, kitchen, pantry and china closet on the first floor and laundry beneath the kitchen. The second story of the residence had four bedrooms, with a bathroom and closet for each room.[204] The sheriff's office was situated midway from the residence and jail, where surveillance of the prisoners could occur. The jail section was essentially revolving pie-shaped cells inside a cage with a central vertical shaft rotating the series of cells. This original design was conceived and patented by William H. Brown and Benjamin F. Haugh of Indianapolis, Indiana, in 1881.[205] A few years later, the patent was purchased by Pauly Jail Building and Iron Works, and the company constructed several rotary jails throughout the country, including in Wichita. Dubbed the "squirrel cage," the revolving mechanism allowed the jail keeper to control the prisoners without making personal contact with them. The Pauly Company claimed the rotary design removed opportunities for prisoners

(No Model.) 5 Sheets—Sheet 1.

W. H. BROWN & B. F. HAUGH.

JAIL OR PRISON.

No. 244,358. Patented July 12, 1881.

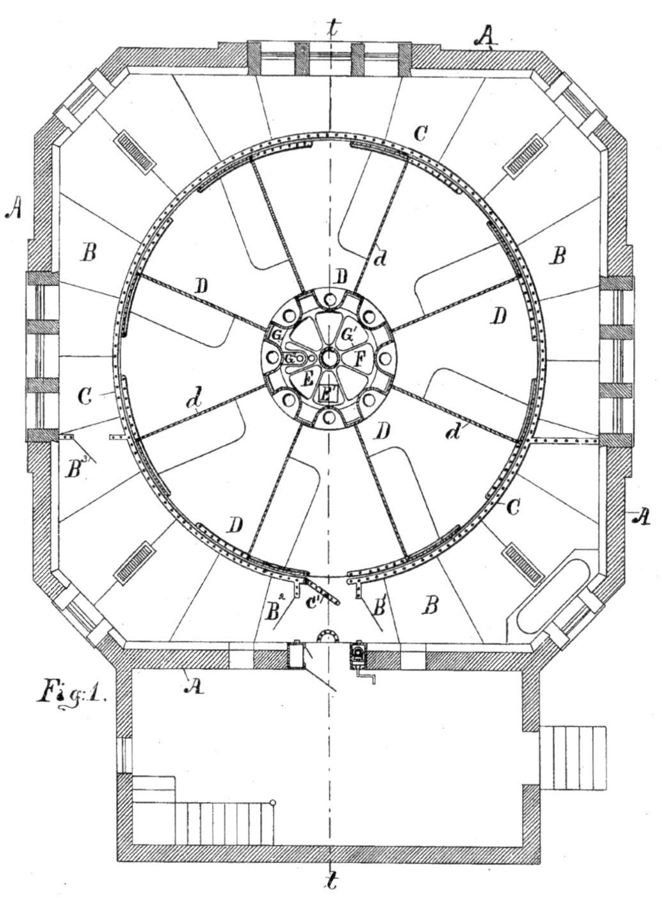

WITNESSES.

INVENTOR.

William H. Brown, and Benjamin F. Haugh, per C. Bradford, ATTORNEY.

N. PETERS. Photo-Lithographer, Washington, D. C.

Squirrel cage rotary jail, July 12, 1881. *U.S. Patent & Trademark Office.*

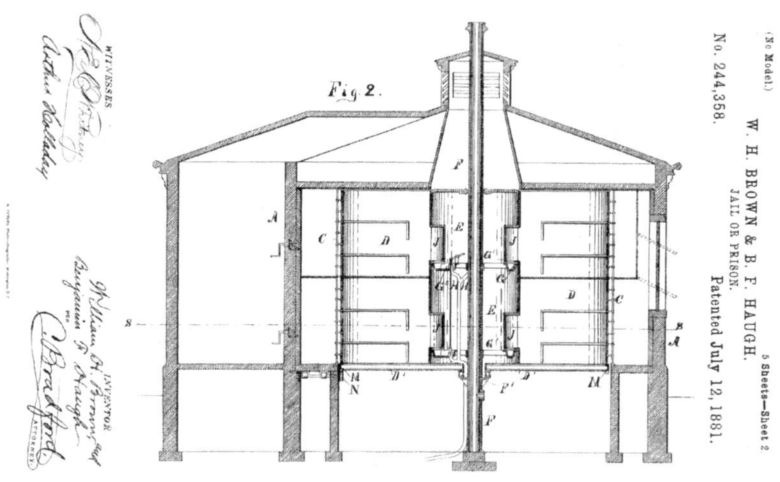

Schematic drawing of a rotary jail. *U.S. Patent and Trademark Office.*

to escape jail because individual cells had to be rotated to the main cell door cavity to be opened. According to the jail manufacturer:

> *As the cell structure revolves, and the several cells contained therein are successively presented in the front of door in the stationary grating, it is possible for prisoners to be put into or taken out from the cells, provided that the door is opened by the keeper, but at no other time is this possible, as all the cells…are securely closed by the grating behind which they move.*[206]

In October 1888, forty-two prisoners in the old Sedgwick County Jail were escorted to the new squirrel cage jail.[207] They first encountered a large, ominous-looking iron door at the front entrance that was intended to make a lasting impression on those entering the building. Prisoners were searched and taken to a cell located on one of two tiers, each tier containing ten cells circulating from a common center. The cells were surrounded with a stationary iron and steel grating, extending from floor to ceiling, with only one door opening in it for each tier of cells. As the mechanism turned, each cell was sequentially presented in front of the door, allowing prisoners to be placed into or taken from the cell. Toilets were interspersed throughout the jail. Shortly after it opened, a local reporter described the jail:

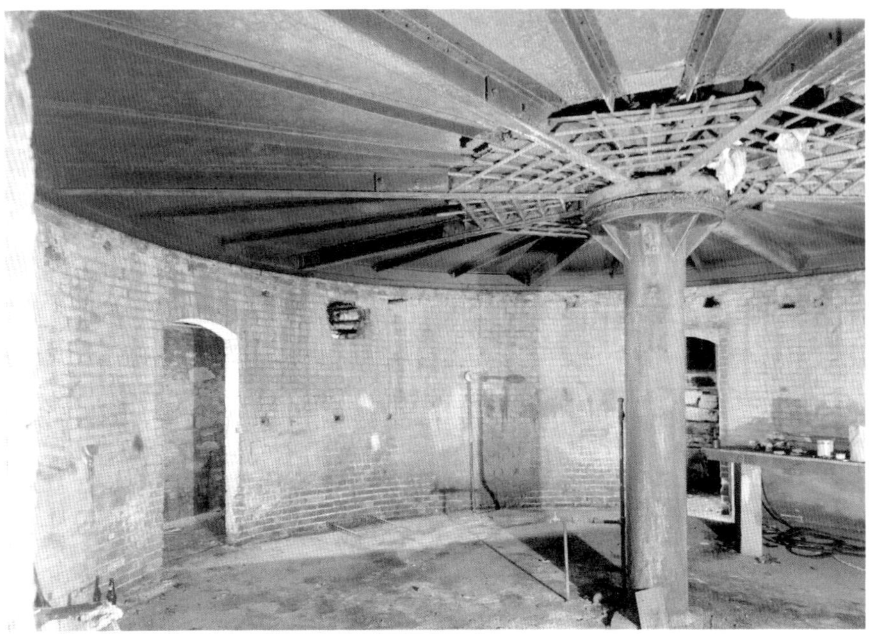

General view of the circular room in the cellar showing the steel support structure for rotating cellblocks at the Montgomery County Jail, Washington and Spring Streets, Crawfordsville, Montgomery County, Indiana. *Library of Congress Prints and Photographs Division, Washington, D.C. Reproduction Number: HAER IND, 54–CRAVI, 1–16.*

> *Sedgwick county will have a jail building superior to anything in the state and in keeping with the wide-awake and enterprising city of Wichita. In fact no better or more scientific jail is built in the United States. The jail is being built extensively in the east. The well-known jail company who has the contract is entirely reliable and is an assurance that the county will get value received for her money.*[208]

In the early 1900s, the rotary jail received a great deal of criticism, much of the malaise pointing to unsanitary conditions. Inmates described the jail as a medieval chamber of horrors, and J.W. Fishman, a federal inspector of jails and prisons, called the Sedgwick County Jail "a sample of the dark ages."[209] On the other hand, local newspaper reports provided a dissimilar view of the jail. In 1919, an article in the *New York Tribune* provided commentary about the not-so-"revolting jail conditions that recall the dungeons of the Middle Ages":[210]

> *As for the "chambers of horrors," it is called the "rotary" in Wichita, and was the wonder of the county when it was built. (There are, as the folder*

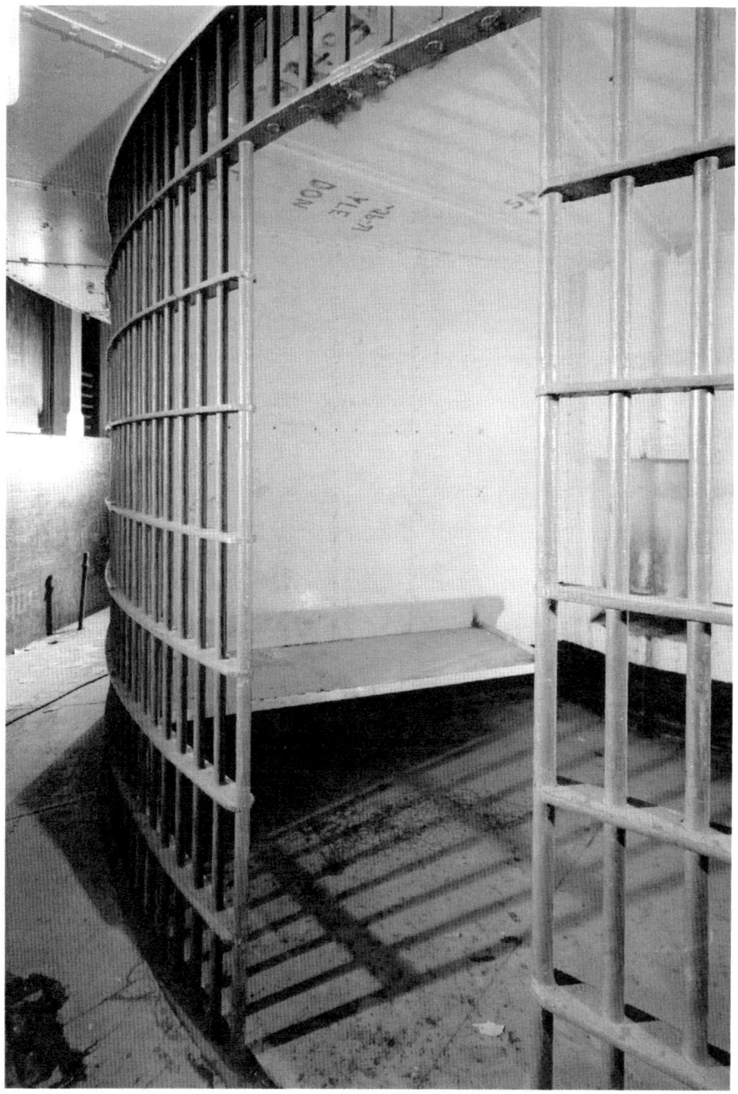

Typical cell in the rotary jail. *Library of Congress Prints and Photographs Division, Washington, D.C. Reproduction Number:* HAER IND, 54-CRAVI,1-21.

states, only two others in the country.) It is no more a torture chamber than any other arrangement of cells. It is simply a very compact and secure cell block. Being clumsy and hard to handle, it is little used. The cells (wedge shaped, as described) are amply large to contain a bunk, and they are not dark, for the rotary is surrounded by bars, not metal walls. They are unusually light and well ventilated, in fact.[211]

By 1916, the thirty-year-old rotary jail had become structurally flawed, and county commissioners proposed a new detention facility, which voters overwhelming endorsed in an election vote later that year. The new jail was estimated to cost $100,000 and would be placed near the courthouse. Ground preparation started north of the courthouse, but construction of the new jail came to a halt because the bond issue of one mill levy for one year required to build the new jail wasn't published long enough before the voting. Consequently, the jail building contracts were cancelled, and commissioners for a time considered remodeling the rotary jail. However, Judge Jesse Wall ruled the jail unsafe and ordered it closed. In 1924, the structure was dismantled, and the era of the squirrel cage jail in Wichita came to an end.

13

THE STEEL CAGE BUILDERS

The period from 1865 to 1890 was one of great mechanical and industrial progress. Pre-manufactured jail cells were fabricated as early as 1859 (e.g., Iron Jail of Lawrence) and began to get serious consideration as a fast response to much-needed jail space. Materials readily available could be used to build the jail's exterior structure, while the inside could be fitted with steel and iron enclosures and heavy locking mechanisms. These cages came in multiple shapes and sizes and, with the expansion of railroads across the state, could be delivered quickly at a reasonable cost.

Demand for iron hit its peak in the 1860s with the increased production of ironclad warships and the expansion of the rail system, both in Kansas and across the United States. As iron became more common, it was widely used for jail cells. While many cells for city and county jails would be locally manufactured, four companies would make a great deal of money and build their reputations as the nation's best builders of jail cells and locking devices. They were the P.J. Pauly, E.T. Barnum, R.C. Stewart and J.H. Van Dorn manufacturing companies.

P.J. Pauly & Brother Jail Building Company, St. Louis, Missouri

One of the first jail fabrication companies to gain prominence in Kansas was the P.J. Pauly & Brother Jail Building and Manufacturing Company of

St. Louis, Missouri. The company's founder, Peter Pauly, was a blacksmith known for his workmanship with wrought iron, crafting his skills by repairing steamboats.[212] Partnering with his brother, John Pauly, the two men began manufacturing small steel jail cages. Later, in 1880, P.J. Pauly Jr. became a partner and then president of the company in 1889.[213]

The Pauly Company pioneered double-ribbed bar and the development of "tool-resisting steel," necessary to maintain a high level of physical security for openings, such as fixed and operable exterior and interior windows, bar gratings and perimeter walls that enclose or separate jail cells and other spaces. The company's 1877 patent, titled "Jail Cells," called for "securing parallel bars of steel at intervals over part or the whole of the metallic surface of the walls, roof, and floor of a jail cell, in order to prevent the prisoner from cutting out a piece of the plate of sufficient size to permit his escape."[214] A similar invention by the company was a method of

> *attaching the sliding bolts that lock the cell door to a lever, by which said bolts are operated, and the levers of a number of doors in a row are connected to a single sliding bar operated by a lever outside the corridor and enclosed within a locked case, so that the lever can only be operated (to lock or unlock the cell doors) when the case door is open. The operating lever, when the cell doors are locked, engages over a staple to receive a padlock.*[215]

The company built jails throughout the state of Kansas, including in Wellington, Junction City, Wichita, Colby and Wakeeney. The sheriff's residence and jail in Seneca, Kansas, which was built in 1879 at a cost of $9,965, stands as one of the more imposing jail structures of its time and features Pauly jail cells and a level-locking system. This two-story brick building was both a residence for the jailer and his family and a high-security jail for prisoners. In the prisoners' area, all the exterior windows had thick vertical metal bars affixed to double-pane, seventy-seven- by thirty-four-inch windows with pulleys and weights. The exterior walls were twelve inches thick, covered with dark red brick. The inside contained three cells (roughly seven feet wide by eight feet deep by six feet high), each sufficient to hold four persons. The cell doors were controlled by a lever-release system in which the jailer could remove a padlock to a steel box outside the cell area and pull the lever that repositioned a locking bar and released the cell doors. Above the jailer's residence were two rooms used for the incarceration of female prisoners and those retained for minor offenses. In connection with the building is a large cistern and facilities for using the water to the best advantage in case of fire.[216]

Prior to 1860, no jail was needed in Nemaha County, Kansas. On the rare occasion that a prisoner was taken into custody, he was lodged in various places and usually under guard. In 1861, after Seneca became the county seat, commissioners erected a twenty- by twenty-foot stone jail that contained four cells: two lighted ones and two dungeons. Escapes from it were not only frequent but also the norm. Like so many other frontier jails, the building was often the focus of mob justice. Such was the case on February 27, 1865, when Miles Carter was arrested for horse stealing and taken to the Seneca jail. That night, around eleven o'clock, a mob of about twenty men overpowered the guard and took Carter from jail. The next morning, his body was found hanging from the limb of a tree about eight miles from Seneca. An inquest was held, and a verdict found that the deceased came to his death in the manner stated, at the hands of person or persons unknown to the jury.[217]

The last execution in Nemaha County, Kansas, took place on September 18, 1869. A former Pony Express rider, Jayhawker guerrilla raider and convict by the name of Melvin Baughn was arrested and jailed for suspicion of murder. While in jail, a local mob set on lynching Baughn demanded the deputy sheriff turn over the prisoner. However, the law officer would not yield, and the crowd was turned back. Ironically, a few weeks later, Baughn, with the assistance of another prisoner, succeeded in forcing open the doors and escaping, helping themselves to arms and ammunition stored inside the jail. Baughn robbed a general store in Wathena, Kansas, to get a stake of $800. He remained a fugitive for fifteen months before he was captured and returned to Seneca for trial. The jury returned a guilty verdict of murder, and the court promptly sentenced Baughn to be legally executed. The condemned man was positioned on the trapdoor of the gallows that had been built in the jail yard. Shortly after 3:00 p.m. on the day of his execution, the rope to the trapdoor was cut, and Baughn dropped to his death.[218]

As Seneca continued to grow and expand into the 1900s, the jail began to show signs of deterioration. By 1905, the floor had weakened, and the brick wall in one area was so deteriorated that one prisoner simply pushed out a section and left. Also, serious health problems arose due to unsanitary conditions in the jail:

> *The floor in the corridor was an ordinary plank affair that was put down some sixteen years before over the brick and sand flooring. Time and moisture rotted the planks. One could take a stick and stir in the mud underneath. The cages had a steel bottom and were set on a cement floor,*

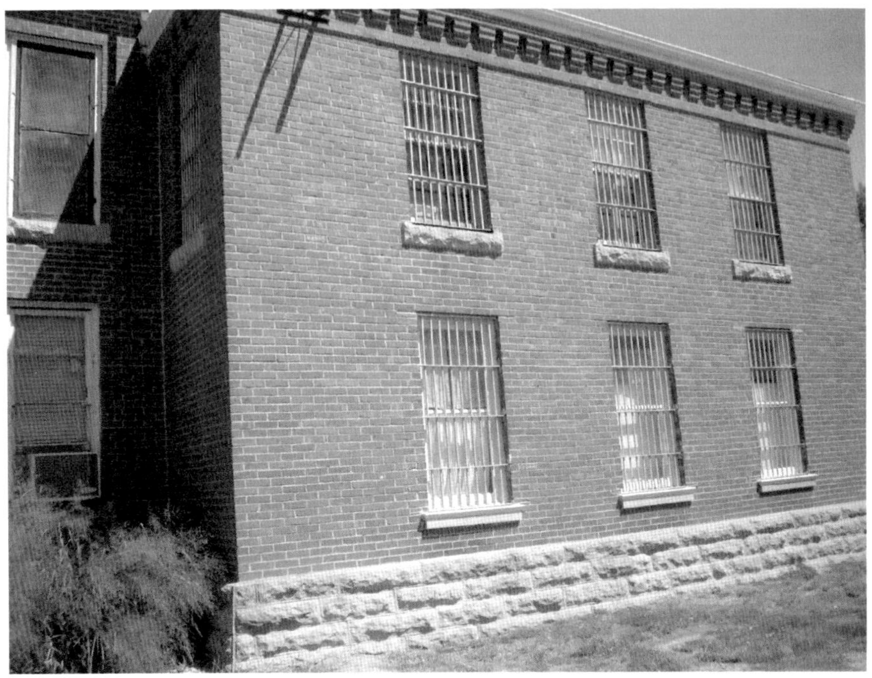

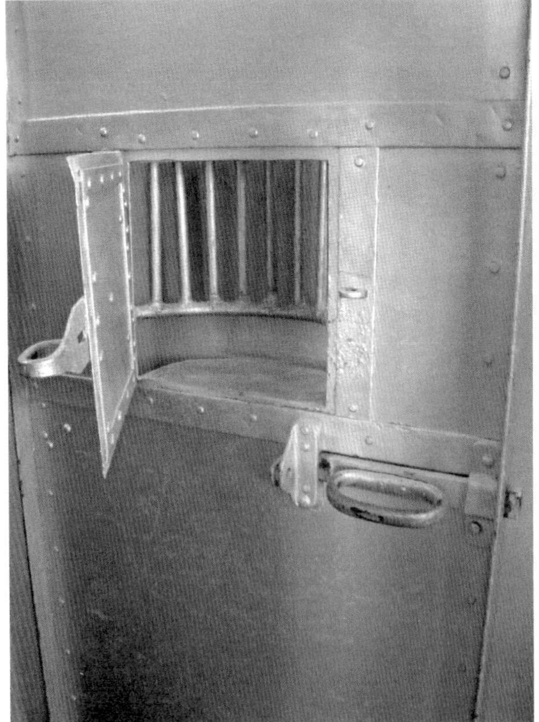

Above: The 1879 sheriff's residence and jail in Seneca, Kansas.

Left: "Bean hole" to cells at the Seneca, Kansas jail.

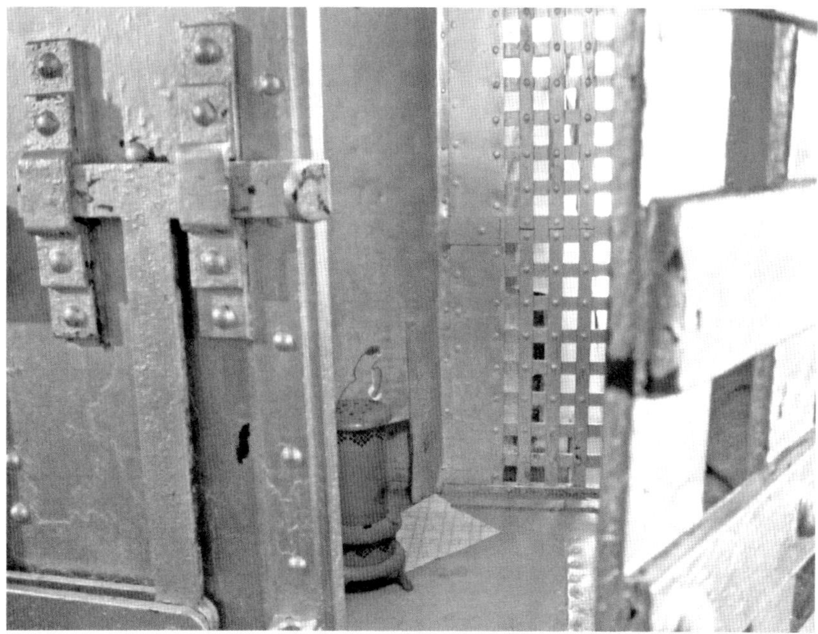

Heat stove inside an iron cell at the Seneca, Kansas jail.

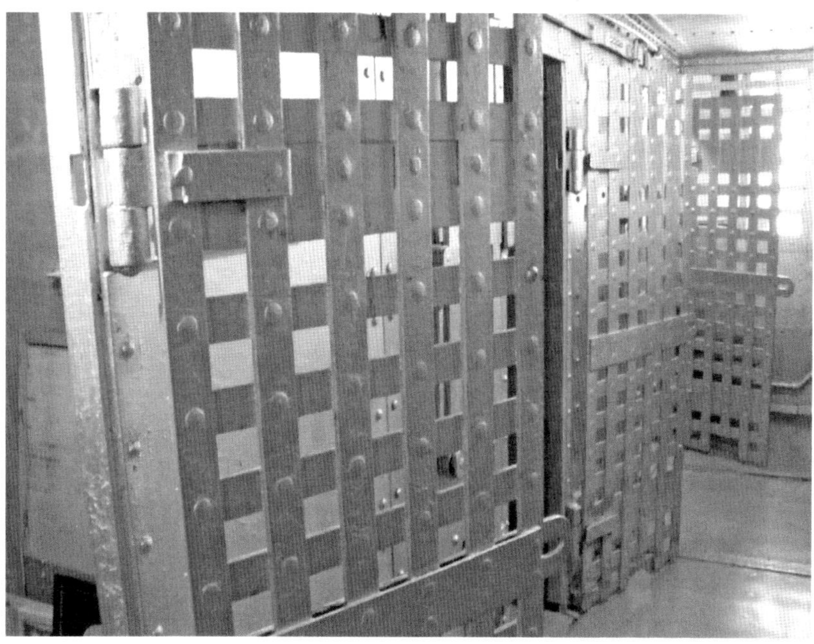

Cells and locking mechanism at the 1879 Seneca, Kansas jail.

> *but the dampness had completely rusted through the steel bottoms in some places. Several prisoners contracted rheumatism while in the jail. Obnoxious gases caused prisoners to feel nauseous. Malaria was reported to be lurking throughout the entire premises. One young man visited neighbors after being held at the hail, his clothing contaminated the house with a foul odor. His best shoes were covered in mildew and he looked sick. He went to the jail the picture of health and youth, and was released pale and sick from malaria.*[219]

In 1907, the Seneca jail was completely renovated, yet less than a year later, a most tragic event occurred when James Lally, a twenty-two-year-old prisoner awaiting trial for murder, was burned to death. Lally was to have had his trial in district court the next day on the charge of murdering Herbert Jordon, a prominent newspaperman who had served as secretary for former Kansas governor Willis Bailey. It was thought that Lally intentionally set his sleeping mattress on fire inside the jail cell. By the time Sheriff William Dennis arrived on the scene, the prisoner was lying in the corridor of the steel cage, his clothing nearly burned from his body. Still conscious, Lally communicated that he was cold, so he lit his oil heater and, in doing so, splashed the oil on his bed. It immediately ignited the mattress, and his clothing caught fire. Lally died in agony twenty minutes later. Sheriff Dennis stated that the stove held not more than a half gallon of oil and that when he turned his attention to the fire after carrying Lally out of the cell, the bedding was on fire in one spot in the center of the bunk. Moreover, with his trial approaching, the prisoner hadn't eaten much and was restless. Both the sheriff and his deputy expressed the opinion that Lally showed signs of strange behavior, but Lally's attorney, W.W. Redmond, maintained that there were no grounds to suspect that his client committed suicide.[220]

E.T. Barnum Wire and Iron Works, Detroit, Michigan

Another nationally recognized manufacturer of jail structures was the Eugene T. Barnum Wire and Iron Works Company of Detroit, Michigan. Founded in 1866, Barnum Iron initially produced ornamental railings in wrought-iron and steel materials for stairs. The company also was well known for manufacturing fire escapes, fences, gates and other ornamental iron. However,

Right, top: Steel lattice jail cell manufactured by the E.T. Barnum Wire and Iron Works Company.

Right, bottom: Iron odorless night soil and prison bucket manufactured by the E.T. Barnum Wire and Iron Works Company.

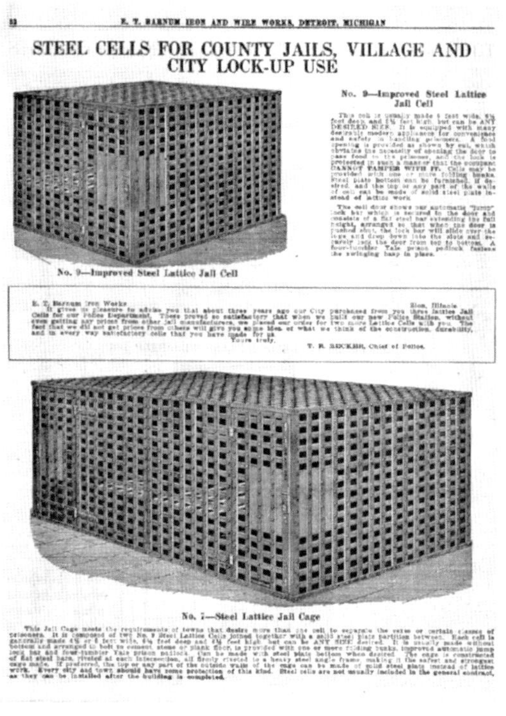

E. T. BARNUM IRON AND WIRE WORKS, DETROIT, MICHIGAN

STEEL CELLS FOR COUNTY JAILS, VILLAGE AND CITY LOCK-UP USE

No. 9—Improved Steel Lattice Jail Cell

No. 9—Improved Steel Lattice Jail Cell

E. T. Barnum Iron Works — Zion, Illinois

It gives us pleasure to advise you that about three years ago our City purchased from you three lattice Jail Cells for our Police Department. These proved so satisfactory that when we built our new Police Station, without even getting any prices from other jail manufacturers, we placed our order for two more Lattice Cells with you. The fact that we did not get prices from others will give you some idea of what we think of the construction, durability, and in every way satisfactory cells that you have made for us.

Yours truly,

[illegible], Chief of Police.

No. 7—Steel Lattice Jail Cage

the most identifiable physical evidence of Barnum's existence during frontier Kansas is its jail cells.[221] In an 1893 special circular, the Barnum Iron Company provides a description of its lattice jail cell.

> *This is the cheapest, safest, and most popular Jail cell made, and every town should have this protection. Usually made without bottom, to fasten to stone, cement or plank floor, with Bunk and Jail padlock, cross bars of Bessemer jail steel securely riveted at each intersection with heavy steel rivets, all securely riveted to a heavy Bessemer Steel Angle Frame. Especially adapted for station houses and villages wanting a strong, secure and inexpensive jail cell. This style is open all the way around, so that the prisoner is constantly under the surveillance of the watchman or jailer. The usual size of the cell is 5 ft. x 6 ft. 6 in. x 6ft. 6 in. high, but they can be made ANY SIZE DESIRED, wither smaller or larger.*[222]

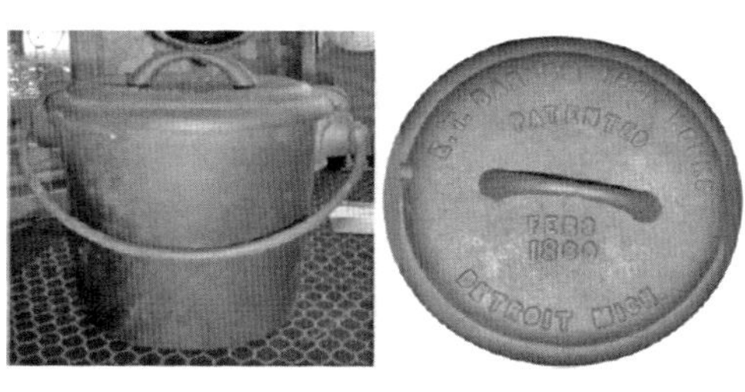

In addition to cells, Barnum Iron patented other jail-related fixtures. Once such item was the 1880 patented odorless night soil and prison bucket. Often simply referred to as the "jail pail," this cast-iron bucket served as a

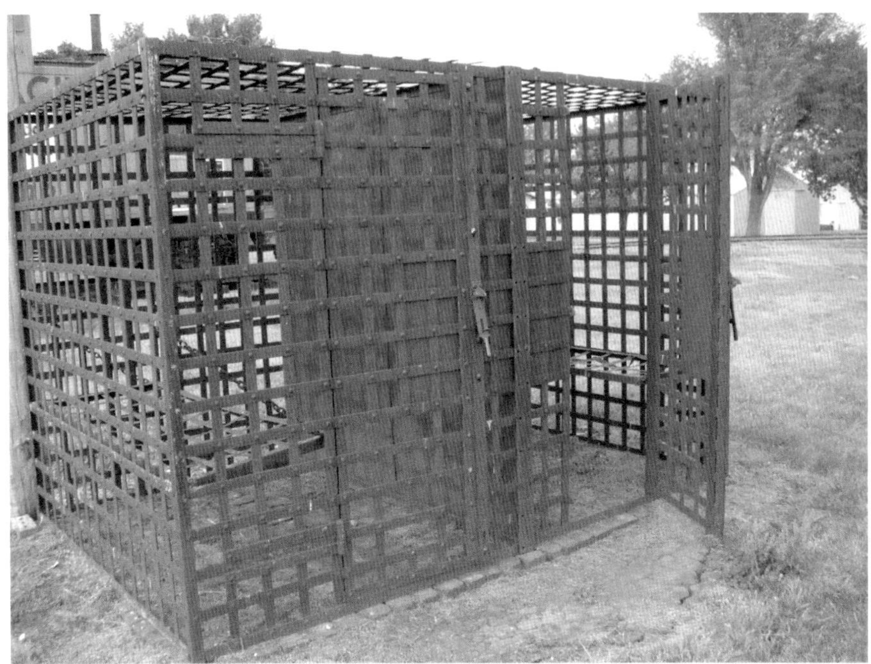

An 1870 prefabricated double cell assembly in Albany, Kansas.

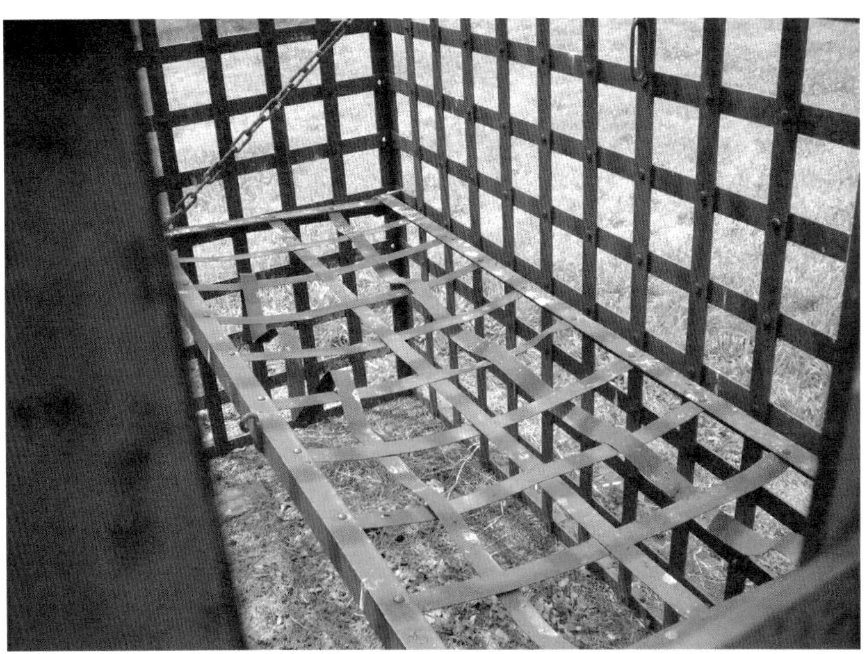

Bed rack inside a cell of the 1870 jail in Albany, Kansas.

portable waste container for prisoners. It featured a bail or handle that could be moved from one side of the vessel to the other, which made it airtight. The bucket could be purchased to stand alone in a jail cell or united with a corner commode and ventilating pipe, which enclosed the night soil bucket, thereby providing a sanitary cell.[223]

R.C. Stewart Iron Works Company, Covington, Kentucky

In 1862, Robert C. Stewart opened an ironworks plant in Covington, Kentucky, and today it's the country's second-oldest iron company in continuous operation.[224] Two of Stewart's sons, Robert Jr. and Wallace, began a similar business in Wichita, Kansas, in 1886. They returned to Covington nine years later and joined their father's business, along with a third brother. They would open a bridge works plant in Cincinnati, Ohio, and a related service, called Stewart Jail Works.

Stewart Jail Works manufactured fencing, jail cells and fire- and burglar-proof vaults. In the late nineteenth century, Stewart was one of the world's largest producers of iron fencing and began making jail cells. The company would pioneer new locking devices that enabled the jailer to open all of the cells at once or any combination of them. An article by George Laycock in *Popular Mechanics* magazine describes Stewart's jail business in the following manner: "Their smaller jails, including numerous overnight cells in county seats and villages, are scattered across the country. In an average year they'll build a couple of penitentiaries and some assorted jails."[225]

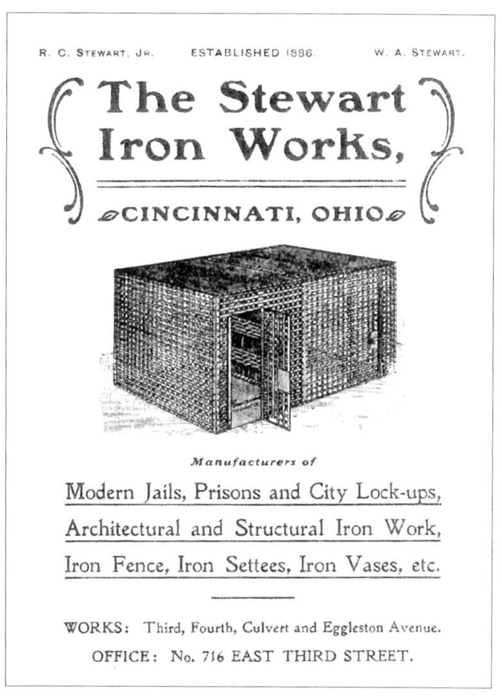

Stewart Iron Works catalogue poster.

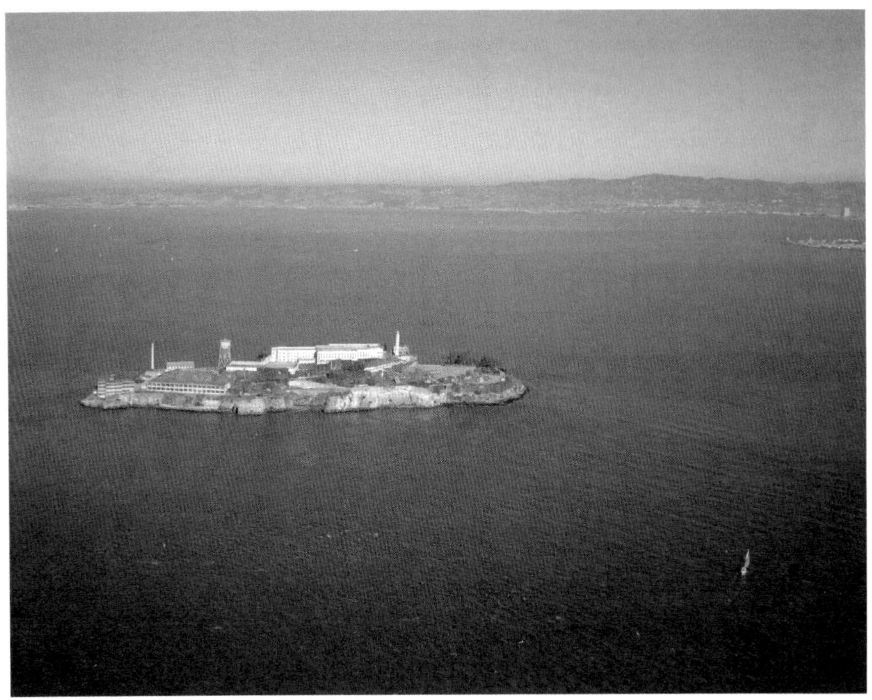

Aerial view of the federal penitentiary at Alcatraz Island. *Library of Congress.*

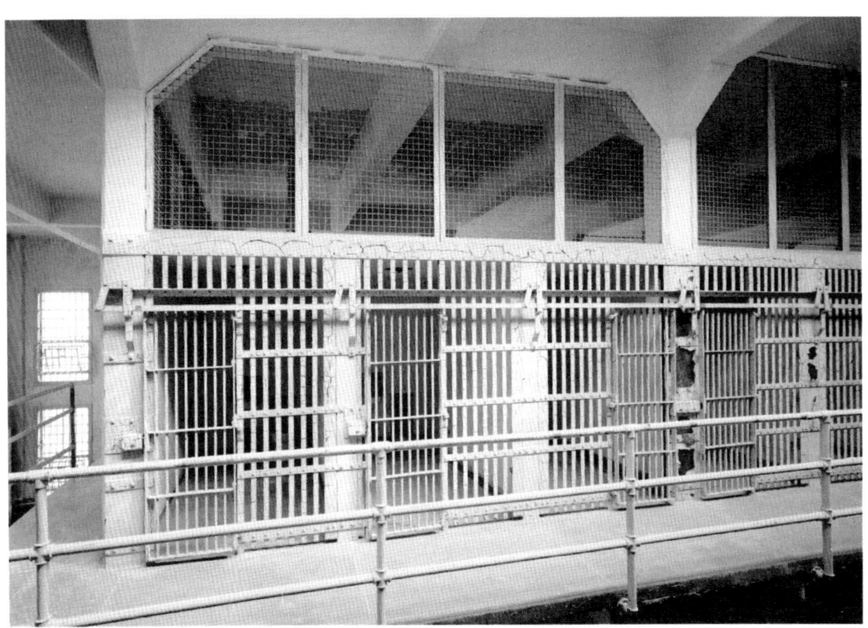

Prisoner cellblock A at Alcatraz Island, manufactured by Stewart Iron Works. *Library of Congress.*

Beside jails, Stewart's engineers were instrumental in designing and building federal and state penitentiaries. In 1891, Congress passes the Three Prisons Act, establishing the federal prison system. Stewart Jail Cell Division produced jail cells for most of the maximum-security penitentiaries in the country, including Atlanta, Georgia (1902); Leavenworth, Kansas (1904); and Alcatraz, California (1904). The company delivered jail products to state prisons such as Sing Sing (1914) and Attica, New York. The jail division was eventually sold to Pott Industries (St. Louis) and merged with Decatur Iron and Steel. It is reported that Stewart Jail Works manufactured jail cells for at least ninety-two prisons and eighty-five smaller city station houses and lockups nationwide.[226]

J.H. Van Dorn Iron Works Company, Cleveland, Ohio

The story of large manufacturing companies that fabricated jail cells would not be complete without including the Van Dorn Iron Works Company. The Van Dorn Iron Works Company of Cleveland, Ohio, began manufacturing jail cells in 1884. As the story goes, the company's founder, James H. Van Dorn, a blacksmith who honed his skills making iron fence, overheard someone mentioning jail cell construction. Thinking that jail cells were nothing more than indoor fences, he added prefabricated cells to the production line. Within a few years, Van Dorn's company was one of the largest manufacturers of jail cells. Dozens of patents were granted to Van Dorn Iron Works for inventions relating to cell construction, locking devices and cell door control systems.[227]

Van Dorn Iron Works secured bids for many prison and jail construction projects, most in the eastern part of the United States. The company built prison cells for state confinement facilities such as the Connecticut State Prison (187 cells), Tombs Prison of New York City (352 cells), Nebraska State Prison (240 cells), West Virginia State Prison (360 cells) and Maryland State Penitentiary (820 cells). Some of the company's large jail contracts included the Allegheny County Jail in Pennsylvania (540 cells) and Hartford County (120 cells) and New Haven County (116 cells) Jails in Connecticut.[228]

The company listed five general classes of buildings that required jail equipment as follows:

> *Every village requires a lockup or calaboose, equipped with steel cells; a town requires a city hall or municipal building in which two or three*

departments equipped with steel cells should be provided; a city requires police headquarters building and police stations equipped with steel cells; every county requires a jail equipped with steel cells, and every state requires a prison or penitentiary and reformatory equipped with steel cells.[229]

The lockup, or calaboose, was the smallest jail manufactured by Van Dorn iron Works. It featured two steel cages, five feet wide by seven feet long by seven feet high. Each cell was furnished with one bunk, and a night soil bucket was considered standard. The municipal jail and police station lockups were similar in design, with both consisting of three lockup quarters, one for confinement of male, one for female and one for juvenile prisoners. The dimensions were the same as the calaboose: a standard cell size of five feet by seven feet by seven feet and window guards made of tool-proof steel. The county jail scheme deviated from the standard size and design features of the smaller cells. It called for cells to be constructed five feet wide by eight feet long by eight feet high, allowing for separation of prisoners by race, sex and age. It also featured witness rooms, hospital cells, padded cells for insane prisoners and an exercise area based on the number of cells in a row.[230]

In addition to the standard design schemes, Van Dorn Iron Works built jail cells for thousands of smaller jail construction projects. In February 1889, the Republic County, Kansas Commission awarded Van Dorn Iron Works $3,940 for cells and ironworks. The jail would include "four criminal cells on the first floor and two cells for females on the second floor."[231] The contract called for the work to be completed by October 1889 and noted:

If the work to be performed is equal to the requirements named in said contract and proved by reasonable test to be proof against cutting with saw, file or other tools usually employed by jail breakers in escaping from jail, then the said jail and structural iron work is to be accepted by the board and paid for in full...but if at any time prior to the completion of said jail by the Van Dorn Iron Works of Cleveland, Ohio, it shall be shown and proven that any prisoner has escaped from a jail of like construction and materials which was built by the said Van Dorn Iron Works, by cutting, sawing, or filing out of said jail, then the Board of County Commissioners are by the terms of the contract, to pay for said cells and structured iron works, the sum of one dollar—said payment to be paid in full.[232]

Ultimately, Van Dorn would be paid $4,153.75, which included its original bid amount plus $213.75 for additional work.

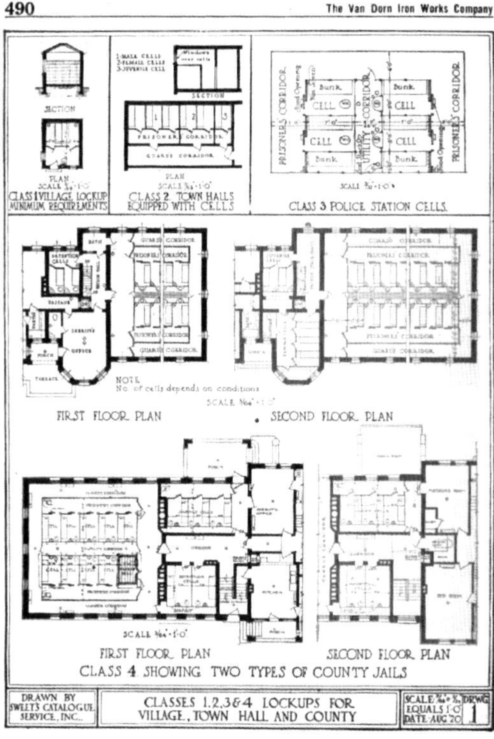

Right: Classes 1, 2, 3 and 4 lockups for villages, town hall and county—Van Dorn Iron Works schemes for jail construction. *Van Dorn Iron Works 1884 catalogue.*

Below: Van Dorn Iron Works jail cell.

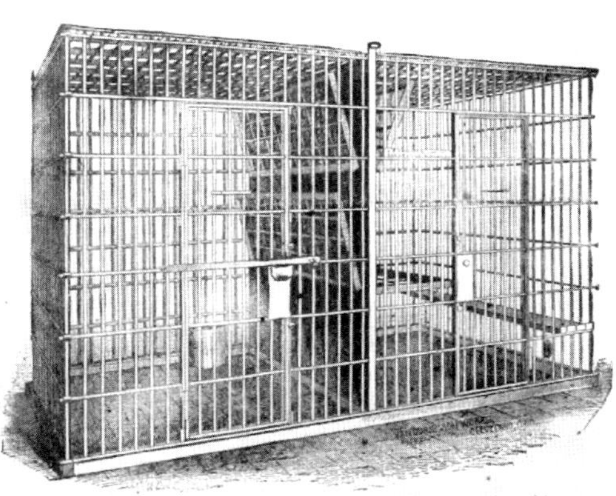

Van Dorn added other metal products to its line, such as mailboxes and metal office furniture. During World War I, Van Dorn Iron Works was one of three manufacturers in the United States to mass produce the M1917 Six Ton Light

Tank. The M1917 stood only ninety-one inches from the ground and weighed 14,500 pounds. It was fitted with a single four-cylinder, forty-two-horsepower engine that generated a top speed of five miles per hour. A thirty-seven-millimeter gun was mounted in the turret. The company would also manufacture armor plates for aircraft and gun carriages for the armed forces.

The prefabricated jail business became highly competitive in Kansas during the later part of the 1800s. The primary reason was the need for jail cells to be placed inside many of the new courthouses built in the 105 counties that were organized in Kansas. If not combined with a courthouse, the jail was constructed as part of a combined sheriff's office or residence and jailhouse. This was much different than earlier times, when jails were standalone structures. To be designated low bidder usually meant a bundle of money to the manufacturing company that was awarded the jail construction contract. The following conversation occurred in 1877 between Peter Pauly and a reporter with the *St. Louis Globe-Democrat*:[233]

> *R: Well, Pauly, how is business?*
> *P: Business is reviving; I have more orders than I can fill, and I am about to rent the car wheel works down there on your ground.*
> *R: I'm glad to hear that business is so brisk, I see the streets are full of people and vehicles, and the hotels are crowded.*
> *P: Yes I am over run, and I must have more room.*
> *R: By the way, Pauly what is your business? I have forgotten.*
> *P: Making jails.*

The large jail fabrication companies were nationally recognized and became well known to newly formed communities in Kansas. These companies made a great deal of money building jail cells, but it didn't always work out for the jail manufacturers. Consider, for example, that in 1887, the city of Goodland became the county seat of Sherman County, Kansas. The town sprang up around the Chicago, Rock Island and Pacific Railroad that had been built through it.[234] When the board of county commissioners took up the business of letting the contract for the construction of the Sherman County Jail, the following bids had been filed with the county clerk for furnishing cells, window grating and doors:

Bid of the Stewart Jail Works Company of Cincinnati, Ohio, for $2,550.

Bid of E.T. Barnum Iron Works of Detroit, Michigan, for $2,550.

Bid of the Pauly Jail Building Company of St. Louis, Missouri, for $3,178.

Although the first two bids were equal, the Stewart Jail Works Company had not presented a $200 certified check as required in the publication notice. The board considered awarding the project to E.T. Barnum Iron Works but concluded it would be cheaper for the county to furnish the material, hire labor and build the jail itself—and "probably get a more satisfactory building."[235]

While smaller townships frequently opted to hire local labor to construct jails, the larger iron manufacturing companies were required in communities where the jail was to be substantial in size and positioned inside a courthouse. One of the finer examples of a Kansas jail situated within a courthouse is the Chase County Jail, located in Cottonwood Falls, Kansas. In June 1871, forward-thinking residents in the Cottonwood Falls Township voted overwhelmingly to support a proposal to build a $40,000 courthouse and jail.[236]

Cottonwood Falls had served as the county seat since the town and county of Chase were established in 1859. When the first log cabin courthouse was in need of replacement, John Haskell of Lawrence was hired as architect, and John Bannon of Leavenworth, Kansas, was low bidder for the construction. Masons and carpenters earned $3.50 a day, while other laborers earned $1.75 to $2.25 a day. It took two years to build this three-story, 113-foot-tall limestone courthouse that included a basement and cupola. On October 8, 1873, the courthouse was completed, and it is the oldest courthouse in Kansas and the Midwest that remains in use today.[237]

The design of the courthouse included a three-room living quarters for the sheriff and his family in the south wing of the building. On the second floor was the courtroom and jail. Its ceiling and floor were constructed of two- by eight-inch oak planks laid on edge and spiked together. The jail included two separate cells constructed of iron and steel bars. The inside doors of the cells were operated by a P.J. Pauly lever lock system from outside the cells. The windows were fashioned with heavy bars, and the main entrance was blocked by one large, solid steel door and a metal bar door. The interior of the jail was painted solid gray except for some of the rivets, which were painted red. The floor and furnishings of the jail were also constructed of metal.

Since the jail space was essentially a small fortress secluded within the county courthouse, one might think it would be less vulnerable to issues involving safety and security. But like jails throughout frontier Kansas, this jail was susceptible to mishaps despite its remote locale. One such event occurred on May 12, 1894, when an angry mob of fifty masked men marched into the courthouse late at night. They overpowered Sheriff Murdock by placing a pistol to his head and required him to unlock the jail cell occupied by George Rose, who was being detained after shooting a teenager. After forcing the

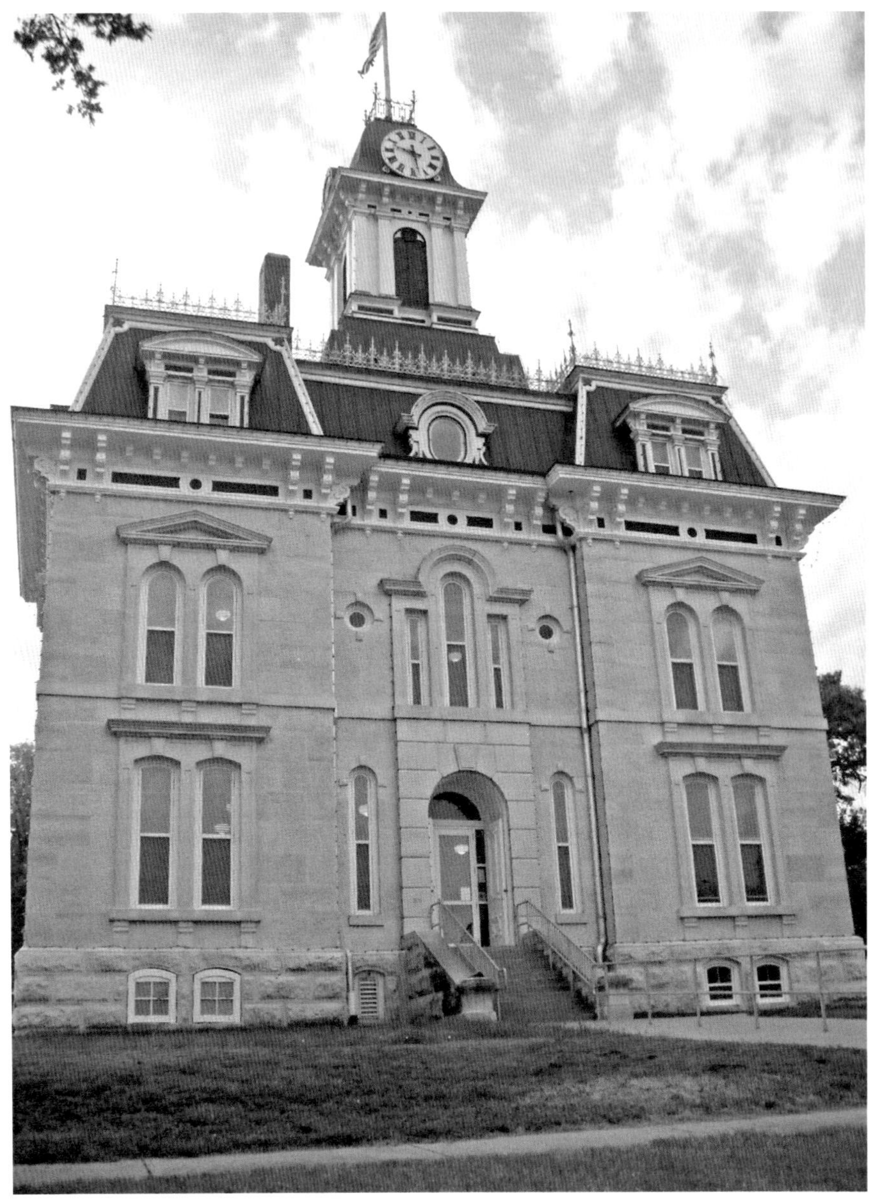

The 1873 Chase County Courthouse and Jail, Cottonwood Falls, Kansas.

sheriff to surrender his prisoner, the mob escorted Rose to a railroad bridge. A rope was placed around Rose's neck, and his hands and feet were tied. Before he was lynched, Rose was asked if he had anything to say. "Nothing gentlemen," he replied. "You are here to hang me, and it looks as if you

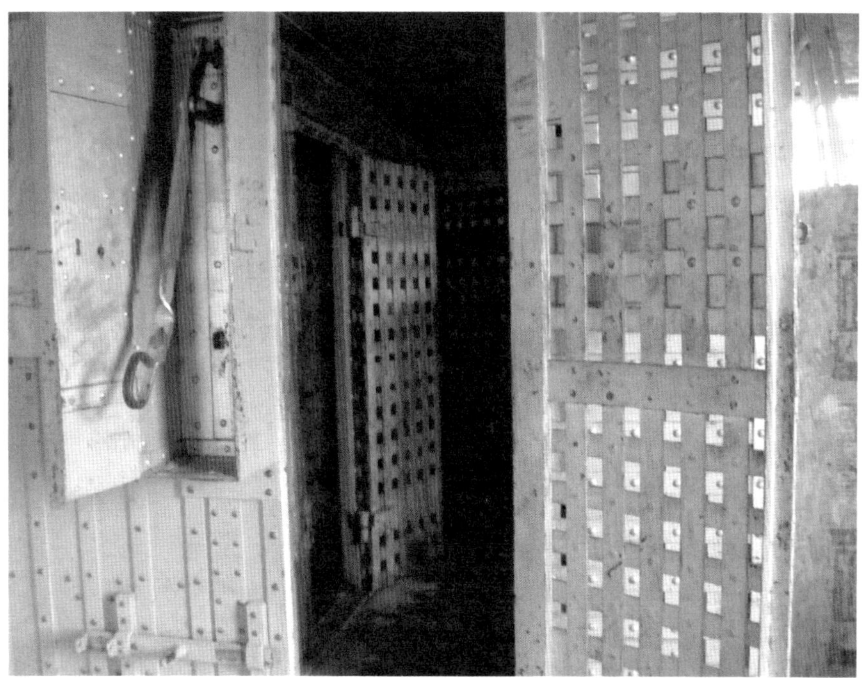

Above: Entrance to jail cells inside the 1873 Chase County Jail.

Right: Locking mechanism to jail cells.

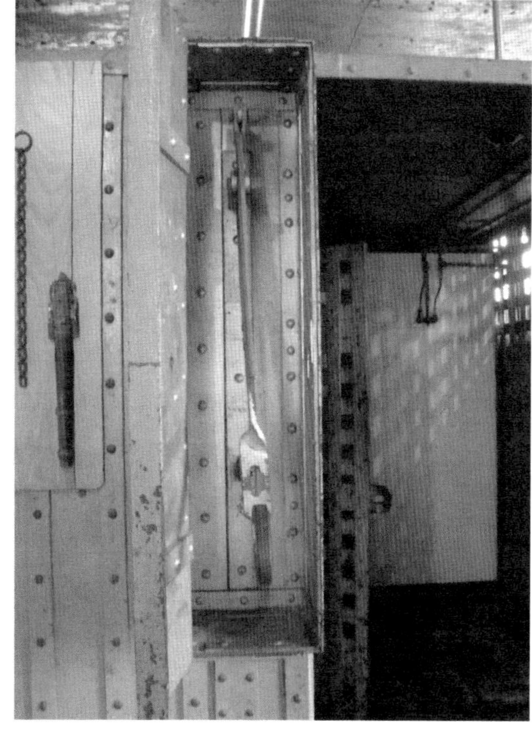

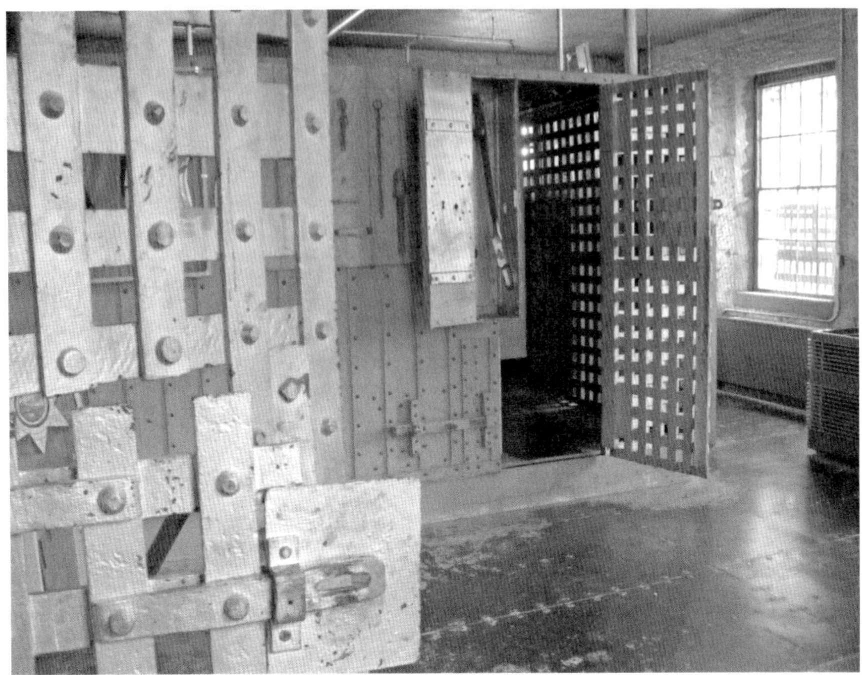

Steel lattice access door to jail cell area.

would do it. I should have preferred to have been tried by law, however." Rose was then pushed off the bridge, falling about twelve feet to his death.[238]

In other townships, community leaders chose to place the jail in the basement of the courthouse. One example of a jail installed in the basement was at the Barber County Courthouse in Medicine Lodge, Kansas, which was built in 1886. The jail was made of hand-riveted Carnegie steel and equipped with four bunks in each cell. It was designed so the jailer could lock his prisoners in their cells and then come out and lock the outer door by pulling a lever in an outside box. Occasionally, the cell doors were unlatched to allow prisoners into a passageway.

Part V
JAIL INSPECTION AND REFORM

By 1890, the western expansion across Kansas had come to a close. A total of 105 counties had been established, and the state population swelled from 103,166 in 1860 to nearly 1.5 million people in 1890.[239] Jails were constructed in nearly every county, and the Kansas State Penitentiary, which opened shortly after the Civil War, now incarcerated, among others, convicted felons from the Oklahoma Territory.[240] The total number of Kansas prisoners reported in the U.S. census of 1890 shows 918 penitentiary convicts, 432 adult jail prisoners and 208 juvenile reformatory inmates.[241] The largest jail populations were found in Sedgwick (55), Wyandotte (40), Shawnee (30) and Douglas (21) Counties.[242]

The customary jail, whether of stone or brick, was a square box whose interior was usually divided into cells partitioned by iron or steel bars. It made little difference whether such a jail stood by itself or was fitted into a portion of a courthouse, for the essential design remained unchanged. Cell furnishings included a table, chair, bed or double-bunk bed and, occasionally, a shelf and mirror. Two environmental distresses were regular features of Kansas jails. First, with security as the major concern, jails were now constructed of iron and steel that created unrelenting noise. The intensity of sound produced by the opening and closing of heavy steel cell doors was annoying to all. For some, the incessant echo produced by the clanging steel and iron set off sleep disruption, stress and other disturbing effects. The second environmental feature was the foul air that was filled with the stench of human waste and body order. Ventilation was extremely poor, causing soil buckets inside the cells to leave a constant and overwhelming rancid smell. A report of the jail in Topeka noted, "Toilet conditions should not be tolerated...There is a hole in the floor through which a noxious gas arises and through which rats come."[243] The overall living conditions in most Kansas jails also promoted isolation and despair. The magnitude of the emotional and psychological pain led some prisoners to consider suicide.[244]

From the late 1870s into the early 1900s, critics of the frontier jails were outspoken about the unsanitary conditions. Dr. Frederick Wines, who was appointed as the first secretary of the Illinois Board of Public Charities and a founding member of the National Conference of Charities and Corrections, wrote extensively about jails. In his address at the Boston meeting of the National Conference of Charities and Correction, Wines addressed the state of jails by saying:

> *The number of what may be called good jails is relatively small. Most of them are unsanitary, owing to their location or to their architectural construction. Many of them are overcrowded, almost to suffocation. They are often horribly filthy. They are centers of tuberculous and syphilitic contagion.*
>
> *The county officials do not know what a jail should be, and the people do not know what their jails really are....The sheriff or the jailer makes a personal profit from crime by charging a per diem for board for prisoners, and by receipt of fees for locking and unlocking the jail doors....We have pleaded for new jails, better jails, when we should have insisted upon their replacement by prisons owned and controlled by the state, thus emancipating them from local political control, with its petty and selfish interests.*[245]

Dr. Charles Henderson, a penologist from the University of Chicago, was asked by the American Prison Association to preside over a special committee that studied the county jail system in the United States. In a summary of the findings, Dr. Henderson notes the following about Kansas jails:

> *The jails of Kansas are not models. Rural and village jails usually have space enough for health, but they are among the worst for vile familiarities of association. The ordinary standard for judging whether a jail is crowded or not is too bad for a stable or cow shed, much less for human beings. This common standard is that, so long as men can find room in bunk, hammock or on the stone floor, with a newspaper for a mattress, the place is spacious enough. This is manslaughter.*[246]

Dr. Henderson's assessment of conditions wasn't endorsed by all, especially district court judges and county attorneys, who were charged with conducting regular jail inspections. Judge J.A. Burnette provides a much different picture of the Sumner County Jail in Wellington, Kansas:

> *As required by law, on the 26th of October, 1894, I inspected the county jail. I interviewed the prisoners in regard to their treatment by the sheriff and his force, and their unanimous testimony was that the sheriff and his deputies did all in their power to make them comfortable; that they had no complaint whatever to make in regard to their treatment in any way. I also found the jail in good condition, being clean and as well ventilated as is possible with so many people occupying, so small a space. There are sixteen persons now confined in this little hole, and it is a sad commentary on the civilization of the age and a mortifying reflection on the people of Sumner County that any human being should be confined in such a place.*
>
> *I might say that I made an inspection of the jail during the April term but the report would have been substantially the same as this and I did not think it necessary to make any report as everything was favorable and I found the jail in splendid condition.*[247]

Another jail examination, this time in Topeka, resulted in high marks and was actually compared to staying in a hotel. During an inspection of the Shawnee County Jail by the district judge and county attorney, the following observations were made about the conditions:

> *The inspecting committee examined every corner of the women's ward and adjoining cells on the top floor, the two decks of the men's ward, where 30 prisoners are confined, with the adjoining cells, and lastly the jail kitchen, a department noted for its cleanliness and good order. After the inspection, the committee decided that the jail was in excellent order, the prisoners well cared for and fed, and the entire institution handled in a way which would preclude any reasonable complaint.*
>
> *While passing through the men's ward, Judge Dana asked one of the prisoners if they were properly fed. "The grub is good, and there is plenty of it," wailed one prisoner, "but Judge, it is just the same all the time at least most all the time. Just vegetables, meat, bread and coffee."*
>
> *The court grew facetious: "Perhaps," he ventured, "a little short cake or pie, fried chicken or the like would relieve this condition?" The prisoner admitted that it might help, and the court, with his retinue, moved on.*
>
> *Jailer Bundy was not present when the inspection was made, and had not been warned of the approaching visit. But the examiners found*

> *the jail clean, well ventilated and sanitary, and will so report to his excellency, the governor.*[248]

Despite the small dose of good news, city and county jails continued to be subject to severe criticism. Knowing that deplorable conditions were allowed to exist in many communities, Kansas governor Edward Hoch canvassed the state to find out whether district judges and county attorneys were complying with Kansas statutes that obligated them to personally conduct at least one jail inspection each term of the district or criminal court.[249] A total of seventy-six counties replied to the inquiry. Of that number, "20 counties made at least one inspection and 45 have no record of investigations. Three counties say they have no jails, and the Ness county jail reported as 'unfit, unsanitary and unsafe, and has insufficient fire protection.'"[250] This probe exposed the indifference to the law shown by local officials, but it would take several years and a new governor before repercussions would follow.

In 1919, Kansas governor Henry Allen ordered a statewide investigation of jails. Since entering office, Governor Allen had received scores of complaints regarding jail conditions throughout the state, especially in the largest counties, which cared for the greatest number of prisoners. Placing the blame on county officials, Governor Allen expressed his concern and proclaimed what was to come if improvements weren't made:

> *It is inconceivable that some of the jails of Kansas are in such bad condition. Conditions in many cases hark back to the dark ages. This is not the result of a deliberate attempt to run bad jail. It is indifference and callousness which comes, from ignorance.*
>
> *The laws of Kansas say persons in county jail shall be given humane treatment under such conditions as make possible reformation. Associating reformation with present conditions in many counties is impossible. It is the duty of county attorneys and district judges to hold frequent inspections. That law has become a dead letter, so far as many counties are concerned. There is no other way to explain this situation. Because of these conditions I have directed the secretary of the state board of health to inspect the jails in every county in Kansas and to report conditions. If jails are not made sanitary and clean, I will direct the attorney general to bring ouster proceedings against the officials who neglect their duty.*[251]

Part of the governor's edict was based on a series of publications by Winthrop Lane about the conditions under which federal prisoners had been held in Kansas jails. Lane's account was based on observations of the jails in Shawnee, Sedgwick and Wyandotte Counties, which he made during January 1919. He described the Sedgwick County rotary jail as the "worst place for incarcerating human beings."[252] The jail featured a leaky roof, bad food, toilets flushed by drawing buckets of water, poor lighting, inadequate ventilation, cracks and crevices in the walls and lots of rats. "At evening, when the prisoners have quieted down, these rats come forth in great numbers. It is not uncommon for a prisoner to be awakened by a rat running over his bed or even across his face."[253]

The first official jail inspections by the state were completed between August and December 1919 by investigators from the Kansas Board of Health. On occasion, the state's fire marshal, Lewis Hussey, participated in the site visits. Overseeing the project was Dr. Samuel Crumbine, a physician known as the "frontier doctor" who established his first practice in Dodge City in 1885. Dr. Crumbine remained a cowtown doctor until 1904, when he moved to Topeka and became the executive officer of the Kansas Board of Health. Dr. Crumbine had visited many types of state institutions in his career and understood all too well the problems that plagued confinement facilities. While speaking to members of the Topeka Rotary Club, Dr. Crumbine remarked that conditions at the city jail were "fierce," an idiom that soon would be embraced by journalists to mean jail conditions were outdated and new jails needed to be built.[254]

As the three-month inspection of Kansas jails unfolded, many different observations were made by the investigators during their site visits. Some counties were reported to have acceptable jails, often described as modern, clean and safe. Others didn't fare so well, especially jails in the larger counties. From these inspection reports, a range of recommendations were made to improve jail conditions. Some of the jail issues required simple fixes, such as replacing the lighting or painting the inside walls white to brighten the environment. Costlier changes were required at some jails. For example, the Atchison County Jail was cited for unsanitary conditions, in part because of soiled bed linens and prisoner clothing. Consequently, a concrete floor was poured in the basement of the jail to accommodate a laundry, making it possible for blankets and bed clothing to be washed on a regular basis.[255] An amplified recommendation for a community to construct a new jail was reserved for the counties of Shawnee and Sedgwick.[256]

14

EXPANDING SOCIAL CONTROL

Critical observations of Kansas jails went beyond the poor living conditions. The character of the jailers was often questioned. The different types of prisoners being detained became a major dilemma for most jails. One of the more colorful explanations of the nature of the late 1800s jail is found in an article titled "The Close and Stinking Jail." A brief snippet of the article offers a glimpse into the character of the jailer and the variety of prisoners inside the cells:

> *The sheriff's jailer, usually uncouth and frequently brutal, was the keeper of a mélange of human beings. Some were first offenders, and others were hardened criminals. Some were beardless youths, and others tottered on the edge of the grave. Others were confined only because they were being held as witnesses. There were those who had violated no section of the criminal code, but who were in jail because of some civil action. Federal prisoners mixed with those who had been tried, convicted, and sentenced and were awaiting transportation to a state penitentiary. According to law, each was entitled to a place to sleep, something to eat, and to medical care.*[257]

Even though a large portion of prisoners were awaiting trial, jails now held sentenced prisoners, insane patients and children. In most communities, it was "common to find the jail the chief means of handling inebriates, vagrants, cases of wife desertion and non-support, prostitutes, and even the feeble-minded."[258] Those sentenced to serve time in jail often left confinement worse off than they entered. Judge Jacob Ruppenthal of Russell, Kansas, noted in a paper prepared for a Kansas Conference of Charities and Correction that prisoners leave jail "worse in body, mind and soul, weaker against temptation, less able to make an honest and reputable living, more antisocial in his nature."[259]

Jails emerged as a convenient location to place anyone who exhibited deviant behaviors arising from mental illness. Their incarceration came on the heels of overcrowded poorhouses and insane asylums across Kansas. Dr. Crumbine would report that Kansas did not have adequate facilities to care for its "mental defectives, hospitals for the insane, Penitentiary, reformatories and School for Feeble-minded all being filled beyond their working capacity… insane, degenerates and incapables have been turned loose in their respective communities, to become loafers, paupers, tramps, to commit petty crimes or worse, and to spread disease."[260] Julian Codding, twice the warden of KSP and well known for his humanitarian viewpoint, notes:

> *Mental defectives were most likely to fall into the ways of crime. In the 85 percent of the prison population, that the towns and cities are responsible for, are the worst and oldest types of criminals. The men, who go to jail from the farms are almost always uneducated, or only partly or poorly educated, or mental or physical defectives. The habitual criminals come from the bright, lights regions. Also, the bulk of the Jail population from the farms is made up of tenant farmers and farm laborers, and among these largely the transient, shifting type of tenant or laborer. Please do not understand me to fling at the tenant or the farm laborers as such. The hard circumstances in which some tenants and laborers are forced to live, the lack of educational advantages and the lack of good, clean, wholesome homes weakens the moral fiber and promotes crime.*[261]

The governor's address to the legislature in 1891 notes, "Hundreds of insane are being kept in the county jails and poor houses for lack of room in the asylums. Though the demands were then urgent, the last legislature made no provision for additional buildings for the insane."[262] The role that local jails played was no longer exclusively the confinement of dangerous people. The exclusive nature of a holding facility for pretrial detainees had changed to accommodate special populations of people who struggled to function in ordinary life and had nowhere else to go. Jails served as de facto mental hospitals for people with psychological disorders into the twentieth century, and this remains a problem to this day.

The jail's role further expanded to mirror that of the state penitentiary by organizing its prisoners into chain gangs. Some prisoners were sentenced to county chain gangs for thirty days in lieu of being sent to the penitentiary for three to five years.[263] These prisoner work crews grew in scale over the years partly because most communities decided prisoner labor provided a punishment more meaningful than sitting in a jail cell. Prisoner labor also meant less money was needed to build or maintain roads. In Topeka, county officials wanted chain gangs to build county roads. They tried to sway political candidates to promote laws that allowed prisoner labor by offering their support for state officials who were like-minded:

> *The prisoners working on the county roads is one of the dreams of the present board of county commissioners and they are almost willing to guarantee their support to the candidate to the legislature who will promise the necessary legislation to enable county officers to put chain gang of prisoners out on the country roads.*[264]

In Medicine Lodge, the public's sentiment was that punishment in the county jail meant more than sitting in a jail cell. It meant chain gangs.

> *The way to put a stop to law breaking is to make crime odious. It is useless to arrest men with criminal instincts unless there is some way to punish them after they are tried and convicted. A quiet rest in jail or calaboose for a few weeks is no punishment for that class. They ought to have a touch of genuine punishment, and at the same time be made to earn for the county or city a part of the cost necessarily connected with the arrest, trial and conviction. Good, honest, hard work is what all criminals dread. When a man is convicted and fined, and is unable or unwilling to pay his fine, let him be put at some useful work, and be allowed a dollar a day and board. A chain gang is no novelty in any of the eastern cities, and in some of them the streets are kept in repair by the chain gangs. In some counties are miles of macadamized road, built by the county, with criminal labor. This works a double good. In the first place, it instills a wholesome fear of the law; in the second place it makes the criminals do work which will partly pay back to the county or city the cost of his trial and punishment.*
>
> *Our county roads could easily be kept in good repair if we could utilize the labor of persons who are supposed to be in our county jail. What if we do pay a guard $1.50 a day to watch a couple of rascals work out their fines? We had better pay a guard $3 a day to watch one criminal work out*

his fine, than to let that prisoner escape without any punishment. The city can put balls and chains on her criminals, and make them do good service in working the streets. Even if we had no useful labor for them to perform, it would be economy, in the long run, to work them at something, even if it was only to dig holes in the ground to be filled up again.

All prisoners, after being convicted and fined, should be made to pay that fine in some manner. If they have no money, make them work. This is the main idea! Let it be generally understood that Barber county and Medicine Lodge have ways and means to punish law breakers, and that class will have a strong incentive to become peaceable citizens. Let's have a chain gang.[265]

Despite their public support, chain gangs never took a firm hold in the county jail system. One reason was the short amount of time an average prisoner spent in county jail. So stability in a prisoner work crew was always in a state of fluctuation. Further complicating matters, admission rates were unpredictable, and serious offenders moved on to prison after conviction. This was much different than the prison populations of convicted persons sentenced for longer stretches of confinement. Understanding these barriers, some officials recommended increasing jail sentences to address the unsteady flow of prisoner labor:

There should be no jail sentences of less than six months. The average should be a year, and the maximum at least two years. If the offense is so light that only fifteen, twenty or thirty days is required as a deterrent, then the offense is so light that the prisoner should not be sent to jail at all....A sentence to jail, as well as to the Penitentiary, should be given with two objects in view: first, to take the offender away from society that he hinders and injures, and that is improved by his absence rather than his presence; and second, to permit of the criminal's training for better citizenship, so that when he goes back to society he will be better fitted to become a good citizen and do his part as a citizen should.[266]

Another proposal was made to turn county jail prisoners over to the state. Relying on information from sheriff reports, it was estimated that twelve thousand prisoners passed through Kansas jails on an annual basis. At least one-third of them served sentences averaging about forty days each:

They could still be handled from jails somewhat as now, but they should all be kept at work when they can work. Probably the warden could wisely

> *be made head of the whole penal system—of the jails as well of the Penitentiary. The complaint now, and a just one, is that to work one or two prisoners from the average jail, and with the average sheriff's lack of knowledge of how to handle them to advantage, would cost far more than their work is worth. This fact has over and over again stopped counties from their efforts to set jail prisoners at work.*
>
> *Under a state system of handling jail prisoners they can be bunched in groups.... Their work, already mentioned, should be out of doors. There is so much public work that should be done that the difficulty will be to decide when to begin. In every county of the state the public highways sadly need all the work...besides simple road work on dirt roads, and better, more ambitious work on rock roads, paved roads, permanent roads, there are bridges and culverts, and work in aid of irrigation and for restraining storm waters in the western half of the state.*[267]

The proposal to increase the maximum amount of time a person could be sentenced to jail never passed in Kansas. Likewise, moving local jails under the authority of the state was never taken up as a course of action. In effect, the push to increase prisoner labor had failed, and laws related to county jails would remain. In its place, Kansas shifted attention toward an emerging national conversation about the need for prison reform. In 1885, the Kansas legislature authorized building a second prison in the state. This facility would replicate the reformatory model, first seen in Elmira, New York, to target youthful offenders who had been convicted of less serious crimes. Two goals could be achieved by building a similar reformatory in Kansas. First, offenders between the ages of sixteen and thirty could be separated from more serious offenders confined at the Lansing State Penitentiary. Second, the needs of youthful convicts could be addressed through vocational training and academic education. Some Kansas Board of Trustee members disagreed:

> *The practical fact* [is] *that our prison population has not increased during the past three years and is yet within the capacity of the penitentiary; and further fact that there is a pressing need for more room to accommodate our insane population.*[268]

Despite this dissenting opinion, a second prison, the Kansas State Industrial Reformatory (KSIR), was built in 1895 in Hutchinson, Kansas. After numerous delays in construction, the institution opened, and the first thirty inmates were transferred from the Kansas State Penitentiary. Over

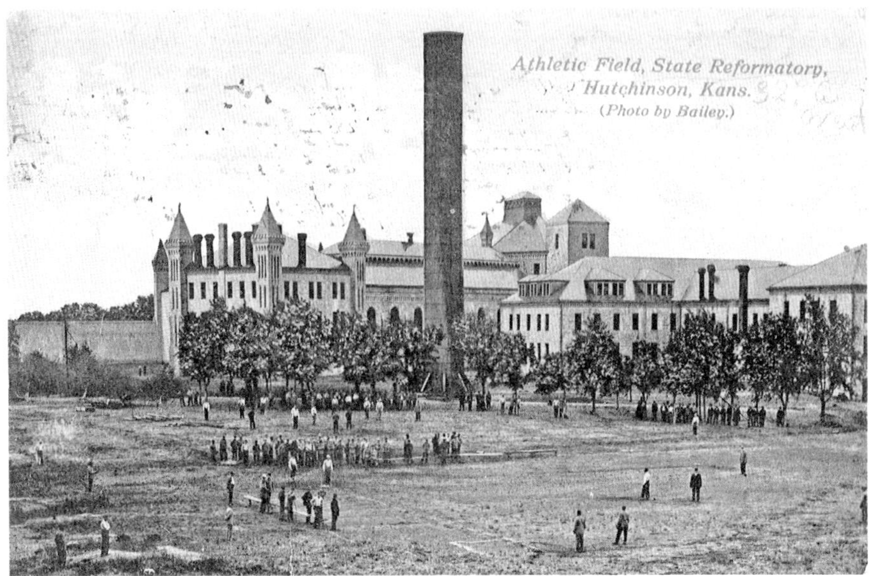

Kansas State Industrial Reformatory, Hutchinson, Kansas, circa 1899.

the years, KSIR expanded in size, and labor remained a central tenet of prisoner reform:

> *When the reformatory is once completed and ready for occupancy, the labor may be employed in producing salt, as coal is now mined at the penitentiary, and expresses the opinion that the institution, as a reformatory, can thus be made self-supporting, without injury to private capital invested in the salt industry.*[269]

The 1890s age of reform set the tone for how Kansas prisons would operate in the twentieth century. The penitentiary would continue to rely on prisoner labor to offset the cost of incarcerating convicts. For younger offenders deemed salvageable, training and education at the state reformatory, interspersed with labor, set the backdrop for "rehabilitation" to emerge as a new doctrine of the state's penal system. City and county jails, on the other hand, would not be greatly influenced by ideas of reform and prisoner labor. The original statutory purpose of the jail—to temporarily detain—remained intact from its inception by the Legislative Assembly of the Territory of Kansas in 1858. Jails appearing across the Kansas landscape from 1854 to 1890 may have grown in size and architectural design but not in sophistication. First made of wood, then limestone and finally concrete and brick, jailhouses were secure buildings that enclosed steel cages to serve as temporary homes for unwanted people. While some of their guests were indeed bushwhackers and desperados, most prisoners were drunks, miscreants and others whose law breaking was measured by the level of their nuisance behavior.

The earliest history of Kansas jails is deeply rooted in the tales of deeds carried out by people who made Kansas their home during the antebellum and Civil War periods. Jails of the 1870s and 1880s, once relatively obscure, began to garner a great deal of public support because they played such an essential role for local justice systems. By the 1890s, changes in the law and government oversight guided how jails would operate into the twentieth century. Jails became bigger and more expensive to operate and continued to be troubled by prisoner escapes and other maladies. Despite this, they have been able to retain their fundamental purpose as originally conceived in the frontier days. That is, jails are short-term confinement facilities that primarily hold people who have not been convicted of a crime. The guiding philosophy of jail remains as well: neither punish nor rehabilitate prisoners. Rather, make certain that those released from jail leave no worse off than when they entered.

NOTES

Introduction

1. T. Minton and Z. Zeng, *Jail Inmates at Midyear 2014* (Washington, D.C.: Bureau of Justice Statistics [NCJ248629], U.S. Department of Justice, June 2015).
2. J.A. Hall and L.T. Hand, *History of Leavenworth County* (Topeka, KS: Historical Publishing Company, 1921).
3. C.F. Harris, "Catalyst for Terror: The Collapse of the Women's Prison in Kansas City," *Missouri Historical Review* 89, no. 3 (April 1995): 290–306.
4. C. Henderson, "Report of Special Committee on Jails," in *County Jails: In the Light of the Declaration of Principles of 1870*, ed. Hart Hastings (New York: American Prison Association, 1907), 23.
5. N.H. Miller and J. Snell, *Why the West Was Wild: A Contemporary Look at the Antics of Some Highly Publicized Kansas Cowtown Personalities* (1963; rpr., Norman: University of Oklahoma Press, 2003).
6. W.G. Cutler, *History of the State of Kansas*, transcribed by A.T. Andreas (Chicago: Western Historical Publishing, 1883).

Part I

Chapter 1

7. T.F. Adams, *Introduction to the Administration of Justice* (Englewood Cliffs, NJ: Prentice-Hall, 1975).

8. R.B. Pugh, *Imprisonment in Medieval England* (London: Cambridge University Press, 1968).
9. M. DeFord, *Stone Walls: Prisons from Fetters to Furloughs* (Philadelphia: Chilton Books Company, 1964).
10. K. Durham, *Strongholds of the Border Reivers: Fortifications of the Anglo–Scottish Border, 1296–1603* (Oxford, UK: Osprey Publishing, 2008).
11. C. Harding, B. Hines, R. Ireland and P. Rawlings, *Imprisonment in England and Wales: A Concise History* (London: Croom Helm Ltd., 1985).
12. G. Newman, *The Punishment Response* (Philadelphia: J.B. Lippincott Company, 1978).
13. H. Mayhew and J. Binny, *The Criminal Prisons of London, and Scenes of Prison Life* (London: Griffin, Bohn, and Company, 1862).
14. Ibid.

Chapter 2

15. *Saline County Journal* (Salina, KS), June 29, 1871, Chronicling America: Historic American Newspapers, Library of Congress, http://chroniclingamerica.loc.gov/lccn/sn84027670/ 1871–06–29/ed–1/seq–4.
16. J. Semple, *Bentham's Prison: A Study of the Panoptical Penitentiary* (Oxford, UK: Clarendon Press, 1993).
17. C. Dunn and M. McCreadie, "The Founders of a Nation: Australia's First Fleet—1788," 2005, http://www.australianhistoryresearch.info/the–first–fleet.
18. Governmental Records and Documents, British Museums and State Departments, London, 1912; *The History of the Convict Ship "SUCCESS" and Dramatic Story of Some of the "SUCCESS" PRISONERS: A Vivid History of Penal History* (Cleveland, OH: Jontzen Printing Company, 1929).
19. S. Webb and B.P. Webb, *English Local Government: English Prison under Local Government* (New York: Longmans, Green and Co. Publishing, 1922).
20. M. Pembroke, *Arthur Phillip: Sailor, Mercenary, Governor, Spy* (Victoria, AU: Hardie Grant Publishing, 2013).

Chapter 3

21. J.P. De Milio, *Voices from Prison* (Bloomington, IN: AuthorHouse Publishing, 2008).
22. Prison Discipline Society, *First Annual Report of the Board of Managers of the Prison Discipline Society*, vol. 1 (Boston: Perkins and Marvin Publishers, June 1826).
23. P. Carlson and J. Garrett, *Prison and Jail Administration* (Sudbury, MA: Jones and Bartlett Publishers, 2008).

24. R.H. Phelps, *Newgate of Connecticut: Its Insurrections, Its Mines, Imprisonment of the Tories, in the Revolution* (Hartford, CN: Press of Elihu Geer, 1844).
25. Ibid.
26. H. Hastings, *County Jails: In the Light of the Declaration of Principles of 1870* (New York: American Prison Association, 1920).
27. E.H. Sutherland and D.R. Cressey, *Criminology*, 8th ed. (Philadelphia: J.B. Lippincott Company, 1970).
28. N.G. Teeters, *The Cradle of the Penitentiary, the Walnut Street Jail in Philadelphia, 1773–1835* (Philadelphia: Sponsored by the Pennsylvania Prison Society, 1955).
29. Philadelphia Society for Alleviating the Miseries of Public Prisons, *Act of Incorporation and Constitution of the Philadelphia Society for Alleviating the Miseries of Public Prisons* (Philadelphia: Jesper Harding Printers, 1835).
30. W. Crawford, *Report on the Penitentiaries of the United States (1835)*, intro. N. Johnston (Montclair, NJ: Patterson Smith, 1969).
31. L.E. Sullivan, *The Prison Reform Movement: Forlorn Hope* (Boston: G.K. Hall & Company, 1990).
32. J. Irwin, *The Jail: Managing the Underclass in American Society* (Berkeley: University of California Press, 1985).
33. A.M. Durham, "Social Control and Imprisonment during the American Revolution: Newgate of Connecticut," *Justice Quarterly* 7, no. 2 (June 1990): 315–16.
34. R. Goldfarb, *Jails: The Ultimate Ghetto of the Criminal Justice System* (New York: Doubleday, 1975).
35. E. Ayer, *Vengeance and Justice: Crime and Punishment in the 19th-Century American South* (New York: Oxford University Press, 1984).
36. T.G. Blomberg and K. Lucken, *American Penology: A History of Control* (Hawthorne, NY: Walter de Gruyter, Inc., 2000).
37. C. Waldrep and D. Nieman, *Local Matters: Race, Crime, and Justice in the Nineteenth-Century South* (Athens: University of Georgia Press, 2001).
38. W. Taylor, *Brokered Justice: Race, Politics, and Mississippi Prisons, 1798–1992* (Columbus: Ohio State University Press, 1994.
39. Ibid.
40. Wiley S. King, Darlington, SC, Portable Jail, U.S. Patent Office and Trademark Office, Publication number US 614008A, November 8, 1898.
41. H.W. Mattick, "Contemporary Jails of the United States: An Unknown and Neglected Area of Justice," in *Handbook of Criminology*, ed. D. Glaser (Chicago: Rand McNally, 1974), 785–86.

Part II

42. A. Roenigk, *Pioneer History of Kansas* (Denver, CO: Great Western Publishing Co., 1933).
43. Anthony F.C. Wallace, *The Long, Bitter Trail: Andrew Jackson and the Indians* (New York: Hill and Wang, 1993).
44. W.E. Connelley, *A Standard History of Kansas and Kansans* (Chicago: Lewis Publishing Company, 1918).
45. Cutler, *History of the State of Kansas*.
46. United States Statutes at Large: Treaties of the United States of America, *An Act to Organize the Territories of Nebraska and Kansas*, vol. 10 (Boston: Little Brown Publishing, 1855).
47. T.H. Gladstone, *The Englishman in Kansas* (New York: Miller & Company Publishing, 1857).
48. E. Thayer, *New England Emigrant Aid Company and U.S. Influence Its Influence, Through the Kansas Contest, Upon National History* (Worcester, MA: Franklin P. Price Publishers, 1887).
49. An Act to Organize the Territories of Nebraska and Kansas, 1854, Record Group 11, General Records of the United States Government, National Archives; Ancestry.com 2009 Database, "Kansas State Census Collection, 1855–1925," www.ancestry.com.
50. L. Huff, "Guerrillas, Jayhawkers and Bushwhackers in Northern Arkansas during the Civil War," *Arkansas Historical Quarterly* 24 (1965): 127–48.
51. J. Balwin, "Officials Say County Jail Faces Overcrowding," *Nevada Daily Mail* 20, no. 102 (2003): 1–3.
52. F.W. Blackmar, *Politics in Charitable and Correctional Affairs* (Boston: George H. Ellis Printer Company, 1900).
53. J.J. Ingalls, *A Collection of the Writings of John James Ingalls* (Kansas City, MO: Hudson–Kimberly Publishing, 1902).
54. C. Bell, "Associate Justices of the Supreme Court Territory of Kansas (1900)," *Journal of the Medico-Legal Society of New York* 18, no. 1 (1900).
55. Thirty-Fourth Congress Report, First Session, *Message of the President of the United States: In Compliance with a Resolution of the Senate of the 4th Instant, Calling for Copies of Certain Papers Relating to the Territory of Kansas* (Washington, D.C.: A.O.P. Nicholson, Senate Printer, 1856).
56. J.A. Hall and L.T. Hand, *History of Leavenworth County* (Topeka, KS: Historical Publishing Company, 1921).
57. R.H. Wilson, *With the Border Ruffians: Memories of the Far West, 1852–1868* (London: John Murray Publishing, 1908).
58. D. Nimz, "Identifying the Earliest Buildings in Kansas, 1820–1861," *Kansas Preservation* 34, no. 1 (2012): 1–7.

59. Mike Yoder, "Vagrants and Tree Shade: Old Ordinance Books Give Insight into Mid-1800s City Life," *Lawrence Journal-World*, January 2012.
60. Ibid.
61. Cutler, *History of the State of Kansas.*
62. *Kansas Freeman Newspaper* (Topeka), February 2, 1856.
63. Cutler, *History of the State of Kansas.*
64. J.M. Peterson, *John G. Haskell Pioneer Kansas Architect* (Topeka, KS: HM Ives and Sons, 1984).
65. R.M. Wilson, *Legal Executions in Nebraska, Kansas and Oklahoma Including the Indian Territory: A Comprehensive Registry* (Jefferson, NC: McFarland & Company Publishers, 2012).
66. E.V. Banks, *Reports or Cases Argued and Determined in the Supreme Courts of the State and Territory of Kansas*, vol. 1 (Lawrence, KS: State Journal Steam Power Press Print, W.S. Rankin & Company, 1864).

Chapter 4

67. J. Leavitt, "The Man in the Cage," *American Magazine* 73 (1912): 540–41.
68. Kansas State Penitentiary, 1863 Annual Report.
69. Ibid., 1869 Annual Report.
70. *Phillipsburg (KS) Herald*, January 22, 1891, Chronicling America: Historic American Newspapers, Library of Congress, http://chroniclingamerica.loc.gov/lccn/sn85029677/1891–01–22/ed–1/seq–9.
71. *Topeka (KS) State Journal*, March 25, 1921, Chronicling America: Historic American Newspapers, Library of Congress, http://chroniclingamerica.loc.gov/lccn/ sn82016014/1921–03–25/ed–1/seq–7.
72. J.N. Reynolds, *A Kansas Hell* (Atchison, KS Bee Publishing Company, 1889).
73 S. Evans, "From Kanasín to Kansas: Mexican Sisal, Binder Twine, and the State Penitentiary Twine Factory, 1890–1940," *Kansas History* 24, no. 4 (Winter 2001–02): 276–99.
74. Blackmar, *Politics in Charitable and Correctional Affairs.*
75. Kansas State Penitentiary, 1869 Annual Report.
76. J.S. Price, *History of the United States Disciplinary Barracks, 1875–Present* (Fort Leavenworth, KS: United States Army Command and General Staff College, 1978).
77. P.J. Grande, *Images of America: United States Disciplinary Barracks* (Charleston, SC: Arcadia Publishing, 2009).

Chapter 5

78. H. Harvey, *History of the Shawnee Indians, from the Year 1681 to 1854 Inclusive* (Cincinnati, OH: Ephraim Morgan & Sons Publishing, 1855).

79. Cutler, *History of the State of Kansas*.
80. E. Barnes, *Historic Johnson County: A Bird's Eye View of the Development of the Area* (Shawnee Mission, KS: Neff Publishing, 1969).
81. J. Svadlenak and Associates, "Old Shawnee Town Strategic Plan 2004–2014: Executive Summary," 2007, http://www.shawneetown.org/Web/ShawneeTown.nsf/vwPDFs/9340767ABE6638248525777F0062BEF8/$FILE/Executive_Summary 072007.pdf.
82. R. Staab, "Local Legend Dubiously Depicts Fangro," *Journal Herald* 63, no. 24 (1986): 19.
83. J. Svadlenak and Associates, "Shawnee Town 1929: Strategic Plan Progress Report 2004–2011," 2012, http://gsh.cityofshawnee.org/pdf/HR/Strategic%20 Plan%20 Progress%20Report%203%2029%20 2012.pdf.
84. *Driskell v. Parish*, Slavery—Action for Obstructing Arrest of Fugitives—Penalties—Examination of Jurors—Peremptory Challenges, 10 Law Rep. 395, 5 West. Law J. 206., November 1847.
85. S. Campbell, *The Slave Catchers: Enforcement of the Fugitive Slave Law, 1850–1860* (Chapel Hill, NC: University of North Carolina Press, 1970).
86. *New York Times*, "Kansas: The Shooting Affray at Topeka, a Private Citizen Kills a Deputy United States Marshal, History of the Parties," May 2, 1960.
87. H.C. Root, "A Few Incidents in the Life of General John Ritchie," *Kansas State Historical Society* (April 1903): 3731.
88. Cutler, *History of the State of Kansas*. See also *The First Biennial Report of the State Board of Agriculture to the Legislature of the State of Kansas for the Years 1877–8* (Topeka, KS: Office of the State Board of Agriculture, December 1878).
89. E. Blair, *History of Johnson County Kansas* (Lawrence, KS: Standard Publishing Company, 1915).
90. S.J. Ford, *Shawnee Town, 1929 Jail Building Report*, CitySearch Preservation, Architectural and Historical Research, 2010. Document furnished by the Shawnee Town Museum, Shawnee Parks and Recreation Department, Shawnee, KS.
91. A.M. Thompson, "Shawnee," *Johnson County Democrat*, September 1926, 13.

Chapter 6

92. *Wichita (KS) City Eagle*, September 14, 1876, Chronicling America: Historic American Newspapers, Library of Congress, http://chroniclingamerica.loc.gov/lccn/sn85032573/1876-09-14/ed-1/seq-1.
93. J.G. Rosa, *They Called Him Wild Bill: The Life and Adventures of James Butler Hickok*, 2nd ed. (Norman: University of Oklahoma Press, 1964).

94. J.D. McLaird, *Wild Bill Hickok & Calamity Jane: Deadwood Legends* (Pierre: South Dakota State Historical Press, 2008).
95. N.H. Miller and J.W. Snell, *Why the West Was Wild: A Contemporary Look at the Antics of Some Highly Publicized Kansas Cowtown Personalities* (Norman: University of Oklahoma Press, 1963).
96. Rosa, *They Called Him Wild Bill.*
97. T.M. Turner, *Wild Bill Hickok: Deadwood City–End of Trail* (Boca Raton, FL: Universal Publishers, 2001).
98. F.J. Wilstach, *The Plainsman, Wild Bill Hickok* (Garden City, NY: Sun Dial Press, 1937).

Part III

99. Brent N. Campney, "Light Is Bursting upon the World!" *Western Historical Quarterly* 41, no. 2 (Summer 2010): 171–94.
100. Eugene H. Berwanger, *The Frontier against Slavery: Western Anti–Negro Prejudice and the Slavery Extension Controversy* (Champaign: University of Illinois Press, 1967).
101. Dale E. Watts, "How Bloody Was Bleeding Kansas? Political Killings in Kansas Territory, 1854–1861," *Kansas History: A Journal of the Central Plains* 18, no. 2 (Summer 1995): 116–29.
102. Kansas Historical Society, "Civil War," 2010, https://www.kshs.org/kansapedia/civil-war/14565.

Chapter 7

103. M.L. Crump and R.E. Crump, *Augusta's Journal* (Bloomington, IN: AuthorHouse Publishing, 2008).
104. *Transactions of the Kansas State Historical Society*, vol. 3 (Topeka, KS: George A. Clark, State Printer, 1903–04).
105. L. Barry, "The New England Emigrant Aid Company Parties of 1855," *Kansas Historical Quarterly (Kansas State Historical Society* 12, no. 3 (August 1943): 227–68.
106. Lecompton Historical Society Newsletter Archive, *Bald Eagle* 27, no. 2 (n.d): 6.
107. Kansas Historical Society, "Report of H.J. Strickler, Commissioner to Audit Claims of Citizens of the Territory of Kansas—J.N.O.P. Wood Territorial Loss Claim," 1859, pp. 590–602, http://www.territorialkansasonline.org.
108. Ibid.

109. Reports of Committees of the House of Representatives: Thirty–Sixth Congress, Second Session, *House Documents*, vols. 142–43, 146 (Washington, D.C.: Government Printing Office, 1861), 1599.
110. *Lawrence Journal-World* May 31, 1982. Sketch sheds light on Lecompton history; "Prisoner—William Berryman—1856," Lecompton Historical Society Newsletter Archive, *Bald Eagle* 8, no. 1 (Spring 1982).
111. T.H. Higginson, *A Ride through Kanzas* (Washington, D.C.: Library of Congress, 1856).
112. J.H. Gilhon, *Geary and Kansas* (Philadelphia: Charles Rhodes Publishers, 1857).
113. *Squatter Sovereign* (Atchison, Kansas Territory), February 3, 1855, Library of Congress, U.S. Newspaper Directory, 1690–Present, December 9, 1856, image 3.
114. *Session Laws of Kansas: The Statutes of the Territory of Kansas* (Topeka, KS: Secretary of State, 1855).
115. *Transactions of the Kansas State Historical Society, Biennial Report*, vol. 4 (Topeka: Kansas State Historical Society, 1883).
116. Senate Documents, *The Senate of the United States, First Session, Thirty–Fifth Congress and Special Session of 1858*, vol. 112 (Washington, D.C.: Government Printing Office, 1858).
117. *Laws of the Territory of Kansas, Passed at the Third and Fourth* Session, ch. 39 (Lecompton, KT: S.W. Driggs & Co. Printers, 1858).
118. Reporter's letter to the *Lawrence Tribune*, October 14, 1856; *Lawrence Daily Journal-World*, "Lecompton Showed N.Y. Writer Barrooms Instead of Churches," August 10, 1957, 2.
119. Lecompton Historical Society Newsletter Archive, *Bald Eagle* 27, no. 2.

Chapter 8

120. *Daily Journal-World*, "Old County Jail Being Destroyed," January 10, 1918.
121. *Transactions of the Kansas State Historical Society*, vol. 8 (Topeka: Kansas State Historical Society, 1903–04).
122. Kansas Historical Society, "John G. Haskell," http://www.kshs.org/kansapedia/john–g–haskell/16761.
123. Kansas State Historical Society, *Collection of the Kansas State Historical Society*, vol. 9 (Topeka, KS: State Printing Office, 1906), 351.
124. Cutler, *History of the State of Kansas*.
125. *Jeffersonian Gazette*, "The Douglas County Jail," 1904, 24.
126. Iron Plate Jail, U.S. Patent Office Publication number US29282A, July 24, 1860.
127. *Emporia News*, "Shall We Have a Jail!" May 10, 1862, 3.

128. *Daily Journal–World*, "Old County Jail Being Destroyed."
129. C. Schott and K. Gates, *Boys, Let Me Down Easy: Murder and Lawlessness in a Small Town* (Lawrence, KS: Cindy Schott and Kathy Schott Gates, 2005).
130. *Daily Journal-World*, "Honor Memory of Ike Johnson, Faithful Employee of County," April 24, 1923.
131. *Lawrence Weekly World*, "Is Old Turnkey," August 23, 1906.

Chapter 9

132. G. Yost, "History of Lynchings in Kansas," *Historical Quarterly* 2, no. 2 (May 1933): 182–219.
133. Nemaha County Jail and Sheriff's Residence, Register # 131–5030–007, April 2004, National Register of Historic Places, Washington, D.C.
134. Editorial by George Adiance, *Seneca Courier Democrat*, August 10, 1905.
135. W.P. Hackney, "The Butler County War," in *History of Butler County Kansas*, ed. Volney P. Mooney (Lawrence, KS: Standard Publishing, 1916).
136. *Erie Ishmaelite* (Neosho, KS), February 24, 1871.
137. H. Frazier, *Lynchings in Kansas, 1850s–1932* (Jefferson, NC: McFarland Publishers, 2015).
138. K. Weiser, *Lynchings, Hangings & Vigilante Groups* (LyCygne, KS: Roundabout Publications, 2014).
139. C.F. Harris, "Catalyst for Terror: The Collapse of the Women's Prison in Kansas City," *Missouri Historical Review* 89, no. 3 (April 1995): 290–306.
140. United States War Department, *The War of the Rebellion: A Compilation of the Official Records of the Union and Confederate Armies*, ser. 1, vol. 22, pt. II (Washington, D.C.: Government Printing Office, 1888).
141. A.E. Castel and T. Goodrich, *Bloody Bill Anderson: The Short, Savage Life of a Civil War Guerrilla.* (Mechanicsburg, PA: Stackpole Books, 1998).
142. P.R. Petersen, *Quantrill of Missouri: The Making of a Guerilla Warrior* (Nashville, TN: Cumberland House Publishing, 2003).

Part IV

143. U.S. Census Bureau, "Population Growth, Kansas and the U.S. 1860–2014, Selected Years," http://quickfacts.census.gov.
144. *Transactions of the Kansas State Historical Society*, vol. 3.
145. Frazier, *Lynchings in Kansas.*

Chapter 10

146. Allen County Historical Society, http://allencountyhistory.weebly.com.
147. *Iola Register*, December 4, 1891, 5, Chronicling America: Historic American Newspapers, Library of Congress, http://chroniclingamerica.loc.gov/lccn/sn8304040/ 1891–12–04/ed–1/seq–5.
148. Ibid.
149. Ibid., December 20, 1878, 2, http://chroniclingamerica.loc.gov/lccn/sn83040340/1878–12–20/ed–1/seq–2.
150. *Evening Hour Newspaper* (Norwalk, CT), "Old Nancy's Brood: Terrible Crimes of the Staffleback Family," September 23, 1897, 2.
151. *Iola Register*, August 27, 1880, 2, Chronicling America: Historic American Newspapers, Library of Congress, http://chroniclingamerica.loc.gov/lccn/sn83040340/1880–08–27/ed–1/seq–2.
152. F. Howell, "Some Phases of the Industrial History of Pittsburg," *Kansas Historical Quarterly* 32, no. 3 (1932): 273–94.
153. N. Allison, *History of Cherokee County* (Chicago: Biographical Publishing, 1904).
154. P. O'Brien and K. Peak, *Kansas Bootleggers* (Manhattan, KS: Sunflower University Press, 1991).
155. P. O'Brien, K. Peak and B. Robins, "It May Have Been Illegal, but It Wasn't Wrong: The Kansas 'Balkans' Bootlegging Culture, 1920–1940," *Kansas History* 11, no. 4 (1989): 260–71.
156. J. Frey, "It Seems that There Are but Few Bootleggers; Anyway, Few in Jail," *Bridgemen's Magazine* 30, no. 9 (September 1930): 533.
157. 123 U.S. 623; 8 S. Ct. 273; 1887 (L. 1881, ch. 128, § 15).
158. Cutler, *History of the State of Kansas.*
159. Kansas Statute R.S. 1923, 21–2150.
160. *Ling v. Jan's Liquors*, 237 Kan. 629, Syl. 3–6, 703 P.2d 731 (1985).
161. Connelley, *Standard History of Kansas.*
162. D. Caldwell, "Carry Nation, a Missouri Woman, Won Fame as a Kansas Crusader," *Missouri Historical Review* 63, no. 4 (1969): 483.

Chapter 11

163. Pacific Railway Act of 1862, 12 Stat. 489, Sec. 9, July 1, 1862.
164. Cutler, *History of the State of Kansas.*
165. K.L. Bryant, *History of the Atchison, Topeka and Santa Fe Railway* (New York: Macmillan Company, n.d.; rpr., Lincoln: University of Nebraska Press, 1982).
166. E. Hough, *The Story of the Outlaw: A Study of the Western Desperado* (New York: Grosset & Dunlap Publishing, 1907).

167. Theophilus Little, "Early Days of Abilene and Dickinson County: Reminiscence of the Long Horn Days of Abilene," in *Pioneer History of Kansas*, ed. Adolph Roenigk, (Lincoln, KS: A. Roenigk, 1933), 30–41.
168. *Abilene Chronicle*, May 12, 1870, 1.
169. G. Cushman, "Abilene, First of the Kansas Cow Towns," *Kansas Historical Society* 9, no. 3 (1940): 240–58.
170. R.R. Dykstra, *The Cattle Towns* (New York: Alfred Knopf, 1968).
171. H. Sinclair, *Wild, Woolly & Wicked: The History of the Kansas Cow Towns and the Texas Cattle Trade* (New York: Clarkson Potter Publishers, 1960).
172. Based on notes of "Abilene, 1865–1871" map compiled by the Dickinson County Historical Society and historian Stewart P. Verckler in honor of the Chisholm Trail Centennial.
173. W.J. O'Donnell, "Unique Construction," *Old–House Journal* 15, no. 5 (1987): 14; P.W. Morgan, *History of Wyandotte County Kansas and Its People* (Chicago: Lewis Publishing Company, 1911); Kansas Historical Society, "Read Kansas," 2011, https://www.kshs.org/teachers/read_kansas/pdfs/m03card02.pdf.
174. Cushman, "Abilene."
175. Cutler, *History of the State of Kansas*.
176. N. Miller and J. Snell, *Why the West Was Wild: A Contemporary Look at the Antics of Some Highly Publicized Cowtown Personalities* (Norman: University of Oklahoma Press, 2003).
177. R. Dystra, "Wild Bill Hickok in Abilene," *Journal of the Central Mississippi Valley American Studies Association* 2, no. 2 (1961): 20–48.
178. *Abilene (KS) Reflector*, August 25, 1887, Chronicling America: Historic American Newspapers, Library of Congress, http://chroniclingamerica.loc.gov/lccn/sn84029385/1887–08–25/ed–1/seq–5.
179. *Abilene (KS) Weekly Reflector*, May 10, 1888, Chronicling America: Historic American Newspapers, Library of Congress, http://chroniclingamerica.loc.gov/lccn/sn84029386/1888–05–10/ed–1/seq–5.
180. Kansas State Historical Society, "Ellsworth County Jail, Ellsworth, Kansas: 1873," Register of Historic Kansas Places, 2003, http://www.kshs.org/resource/national_register/nominationsNRDB/Ellsworth_1873EllsworthCoJailSR.pdf.
181. *Weekly Kansas Chief* (Troy, KS), July 20, 1882, Chronicling America: Historic American Newspapers, Library of Congress, http://chroniclingamerica.loc.gov/lccn/sn82015484/1882–07–20/ed–1/seq–2; *Saline County Journal* (Salina, KS), July 13, 1882, Chronicling America: Historic American Newspapers, Library of Congress, http://chroniclingamerica.loc.gov/lccn/sn84027670/ 1882–07–13/ed–1/seq–2.
182. *Saline County Journal*, September 7, 1882, Chronicling America: Historic American Newspapers, Library of Congress, http://chroniclingamerica.loc.gov/lccn/sn84027670/1882–09–07/ed–1/seq–2.

183. *Kansas Semi Weekly Capital*, April 23, 1897.
184. *Topeka (KS) State Journal*, September 17, 1909, Chronicling America: Historic American Newspapers, Library of Congress, http://chroniclingamerica.loc.gov/lccn/sn82016014/1909–09–17/ed–1/seq–5.
185. United States Department of the Interior, "Ellsworth Downtown Historic District," National Register of Historic Places, http://focus.nps.gov/pdfhost/docs/NRHP/Text/07001065.pdf.
186. *Globe–Republican* (Dodge City, KS), August 30, 1900, Chronicling America: Historic American Newspapers, Library of Congress, http://chroniclingamerica.loc.gov/lccn/sn84029853/1900–08–30/ed–1/seq–5.
187. Cutler, *History of the State of Kansas*.
188. *Dodge City (KS) Times*, October 6, 1877, Chronicling America: Historic American Newspapers, Library of Congress, http://chroniclingamerica.loc.gov/lccn/sn84029838/1877–10–06/ed–1/seq–4.
189. Ibid., October 14, 1876, http://chroniclingamerica.loc.gov/lccn/sn84029838/1876–10–14/ed–1/seq–1.
190. Ibid., November 10, 1877, http://chroniclingamerica.loc.gov/lccn/sn84029838/1877–11–10/ed–1/seq–1.
191. Ibid., October 6, 1877, http://chroniclingamerica.loc.gov/lccn/sn84029838/1877–10–06/ed–1/seq–4.
192. Ibid., April 26, 1883, http://chroniclingamerica.loc.gov/lccn/sn84029838/1883–04–26/ed–1/seq–1.
193. Ibid.
194. Ibid., May 15, 1884, http://chroniclingamerica.loc.gov/lccn/sn84029838/1884–05–15/ed–1/seq–4.
195. *Barbour County Index* (Medicine Lodge, KS), July 28, 1882, Chronicling America: Historic American Newspapers, Library of Congress, http://chroniclingamerica.loc.gov/lccn/sn82015080/1882–07–28/ed–1/seq–5.
196. *Barton County Democrat* (Great Bend, KS), March 15, 1907, Chronicling America: Historic American Newspapers, Library of Congress, http://chroniclingamerica.loc.gov/lccn/sn83040198/1907–03–15/ed–1/seq–2.
197. C.K. Hutson, "Texas Fever in Kansas, 1866–1930," *Agricultural History* 68, no. 1 (1994): 74–104.
198. Dykstra, *Cattle Towns*.

Chapter 12

199. "Another Use for a Printing Office," *Kansas Historical Quarterly* 10, no. 27 (1941): 102.
200. *Emporia (KS) News*, August 21, 1874, Chronicling America: Historic American Newspapers, Library of Congress, http://chroniclingamerica.loc.gov/lccn/sn82016419/1874–08–21/ed–1/seq–2.

201. *Leavenworth (KS) Weekly Times*, July 22, 1875, Chronicling America: Historic American Newspapers, Library of Congress, http://chroniclingamerica.loc.gov/lccn/sn84027691/1875–07–22/ed–1/seq–1.
202. *Wichita (KS) Eagle*, February 27, 1885, Chronicling America: Historic American Newspapers, Library of Congress, http://chroniclingamerica.loc.gov/lccn/sn85032575/1885–02–27/ed–1/seq–1.
203. Ibid., May 20, 1888, http://chroniclingamerica.loc.gov/lccn/sn85032490/1888–05–20/ed–1/seq–5.
204. Ibid., April 29, 1888, http://chroniclingamerica.loc.gov/lccn/sn85032490/1888–04–29/ed–1/seq–5.
205. Jail or Prison, U.S. Patent Office Publication Number US244358A, July 12, 1881.
206. P. Pauly and J. Ligon, *Illustrative Descriptive Catalogue of Steel Jail Cells and Other Steel and Iron Work for County Jails and Other Prisons* (St. Louis, MO: Pauly Jail Building and Manufacturing Co., 1885).
207. *Wichita Eagle*, October 17, 1888, Chronicling America: Historic American Newspapers, Library of Congress, http://chroniclingamerica.loc.gov/lccn/sn85032490/1888–10–17/ed–1/seq–5.
208. Ibid., February 27, 1885.
209. *Topeka (KS) State Journal*, April 22, 1919, Chronicling America: Historic American Newspapers, Library of Congress, http://chroniclingamerica.loc.gov/lccn/sn82016014/1919–04–22/ed–1/seq–3.
210. *New–York Tribune*, March 2, 1919, Chronicling America: Historic American Newspapers, Library of Congress, http://chroniclingamerica.loc.gov/lccn/sn83030214/1919–03–02/ed–1/seq–57.
211. Ibid.

Chapter 13

212. "Pauly Jail Building Company Celebrates 150 Years," *Ironmaker* 106, no. 6 (2006): 2–3.
213. D. Tolzmann and W. Beck, *The German Element in St. Louis: A Translation from German of Ernst D. Kargau's St. Louis in Former Years: A Commemorative History of the German Element* (Baltimore, MD: Clearfield Publishing, 2000).
214. Improvement in Jail-cells, U.S. Patent & Trademark Office. Publication number US197887A, December 4, 1877.
215. Improvement in Bolts for Doors of Jail-cells, U.S. Patent & Trademark Office Number US 155105A, September 15, 1874.
216. Nemaha County Jail and Sheriff's Residence, Register # 131–5030–007.
217. Cutler, *History of the State of Kansas*.
218. R.M. Wilson, *Legal Executions in Nebraska, Kansas and Oklahoma Including the Indian Territory: A Comprehensive Registry* (Jefferson, NC: McFarland Publishing, 2012).

219. R. Tennel, *History of Nemaha County, Kansas* (Lawrence, KS: Standard Publishing Company, 1916).
220. *Topeka State Journal*, "Burned to Death: End Comes to James Lally by Fire in the Seneca Jail," April 18, 1908, Chronicling America: Historic American Newspapers, Library of Congress, http://chroniclingamerica.loc.gov/lccn/sn82016014/1908-04-18/ed-1/seq-9. See also *Shawnee (OK) News*, April 18, 1908.
221. *No. 770 Hardware Catalogue* (Detroit, MI: E.T. Barnum Iron & Wire Works, 1930).
222. E.T. Barnum, *Special Circular of Jail Work*, 1893, https://archive.org/details/specialcircularo00etba.
223. Ibid.
224. *Cincinnati Magazine*, April 2003, 135, https://books.google.com/books?id=S-sCAAAAMBAJ&pg=PA135#v=onepage&q&f=false.
225. G. Laycock, "Big Boom in Jails," *Popular Mechanics* 103, no. 3 (March 1955): 141–44.
226. S. Jobert, *The Encyclopedia of Northern Kentucky*, eds. P. Tenkotte and J. Claypool (Lexington: University of Kentucky Press, 2009).
227. W. Coates, *A History of Cuyahoga County and the City of Cleveland* (New York: American Historical Society, 1924).
228. G.F. Wright, *Representative Citizens of Ohio* (Cleveland, OH: Memorial Publishing Company, 1917).
229. Sweet's Catalogue Service, *Sweet's Architectural Catalogue, Fifth Annual Edition* (New York: William Green Publisher, 1920).
230. Ibid.
231. I.O. Savage, *A History of Republic County, Kansas: Embracing a Full and Complete Account* (Beloit, KS: Jones & Chubbic, 1901).
232. Ibid.
233. *Emporia (KS) News*, October 26, 1877, Chronicling America: Historic American Newspapers, Library of Congress, http://chroniclingamerica.loc.gov/lccn/sn82016419/1877-10-26/ed-1/seq-4.
234. Blackmar, *Politics in Charitable and Correctional Affairs*
235. *Goodland (KS) Republic*, April 26, 1907, image 3, Chronicling America: Historic American Newspapers, Library of Congress, http://chroniclingamerica.loc.gov/lccn/sn85030821/1907-04-26/ed-1/seq-3.
236. *Emporia News*, June 2, 1871, Chronicling America: Historic American Newspapers, Library of Congress, http://chroniclingamerica.loc.gov/lccn/sn82016419/1871-06-02/ed-1/seq-1.
237. Cutler, *History of the State of Kansas*.
238. *Butler (MO) Weekly Times*, May 17, 1894, Chronicling America: Historic American Newspapers, Library of Congress, http://chroniclingamerica.loc.gov/lccn/sn89066489/1894-05-17/ed-1/seq-4.

Part V

239. U.S. Census Bureau, "Population of States and Counties of the United States: 1790–1990 (PB96–119060)" and "1990 Census of Population and Housing, Population and Housing Units Counts: Kansas (CPH–2–18)," http://www.census.gov/population/www/censusdata/hiscendata.html.
240. *Phillipsburg Herald*, January 22, 1891.
241. F. Wines, *Report on Crime, Pauperism, and Benevolence in the United States at the Eleventh Census: 1890*, pt. 2 (Washington, D.C.: Government Printing Office, 1895).
242. Ibid.
243. *Topeka State Journal*, November 19, 1914, Chronicling America: Historic American Newspapers, Library of Congress, http://chroniclingamerica.loc.gov/lccn/sn82016014/1914–11–19/ed–1/seq–6.
244. See *Western Kansas World* (WaKeeney, KS), July 6, 1907, Chronicling America: Historic American Newspapers, Library of Congress, http://chroniclingamerica.loc.gov/lccn/sn82015485/1907–07–06/ed–1/seq–2; *Meade County News* (Meade, KS), February 13, 1913, Chronicling America: Historic American Newspapers, Library of Congress, http://chroniclingamerica.loc.gov/lccn/sn85030287/1913–02–13/ed–1/seq–7; *Abilene Weekly Reflector*, October 16, 1919, Chronicling America: Historic American Newspapers, Library of Congress, http://chroniclingamerica.loc.gov/lccn/sn84029386/1919–10–16/ed–1/seq–6.
245. *American Prison Association Semi-Centennial, 1870–1920: County Jails* (1920, rpr., London: Forgotten Books, n.d.).
246. Ibid.
247. *People's Voice* (Wellington, KS), January 17, 1895, Chronicling America: Historic American Newspapers, Library of Congress, http://chroniclingamerica.loc.gov/lccn/sn85032801/1895–01–17/ed–1/seq–5.
248. *Topeka State Journal*, April 27, 1908, Chronicling America: Historic American Newspapers, Library of Congress, http://chroniclingamerica.loc.gov/lccn/sn82016014/1908–04–27/ed–1/seq–8.
249. Ibid., April 23, 1908, http://chroniclingamerica.loc.gov/lccn/sn82016014/1908–04–23/ed–1/seq–7. See
also Fifteenth Annual Report of the State Board of Health, "Inspection of Jails," *Gen. Star* 2, no. 132 (1897): 76.
250. *Chanute (KS) Times*, May 8, 1908, Chronicling America: Historic American Newspapers, Library of Congress, http://chroniclingamerica.loc.gov/lccn/sn85030529/1908–05–08/ed–1/seq–7.
251. *Topeka State Journal*, August 4, 1919, Chronicling America: Historic American Newspapers, Library of Congress, http://chroniclingamerica.loc.gov/lccn/sn82016014/1919–08–04/ed–1/seq–1.

252. W. Lane, *Uncle Sam, Jailer: A Study of the Conditions of Federal Prisoners in Kansas Jails* (New York: National Civil Liberties Bureau, 1919).
253. Ibid.
254. *Topeka State Journal*, November 19, 1914, Chronicling America: Historic American Newspapers, Library of Congress, http://chroniclingamerica.loc.gov/lccn/sn82016014/1914-11-19/ed-1/seq-6.
255. Ibid., June 20, 1913, http://chroniclingamerica.loc.gov/lccn/sn82016014/1913-06-20/ed-1/seq-10.
256. Ibid., August 19, 1919, http://chroniclingamerica.loc.gov/lccn/sn82016014/1919-08-09/ed-1/seq-14.

Chapter 14

257. Philip D. Jordan, "The Close and Stinking Jail," *Pacific Northwest Quarterly* 60, no. 1 (January 1969): 1–9.
258. *American Prison Association Semi-Centennial.*
259. *Proceedings of the Sixteenth Annual Session of the Kansas Conference of Charities and Correction: Lawrence, Kansas* (Topeka: Kansas State Printing, November 18–19, 1915).
260. *Tenth Biennial Report: Being the Thirty-Fifth and Thirty-Sixth Annual Reports of the State Board of Health* (Topeka: Kansas State Printing Office, 1920).
261. *Abilene Weekly Reflector* (Abilene, KS), May 19, 1921, Chronicling America: Historic American Newspapers, Library of Congress, http://chroniclingamerica.loc.gov/lccn/sn84029386/1921-05-19/ed-1/seq-6.
262. *Phillipsburg Herald*, January 26, 1891, Chronicling America: Historic American Newspapers, Library of Congress, http://chroniclingamerica.loc.gov/lccn/sn85029677/1891-01-22/ed-1/seq-9.
263. *Topeka State Journal*, September 20, 1897, Chronicling America: Historic American Newspapers, Library of Congress, http://chroniclingamerica.loc.gov/lccn/sn82016014/1897-09-20/ed-1/seq-8.
264. Ibid., July 13, 1910, Chronicling America: Historic American Newspapers, Library of Congress, http://chroniclingamerica.loc.gov/lccn/sn82016014/1910-07-13/ed-1/seq-6.
265. *Barbour County Index* (Medicine Lodge, KS), August 27, 1886, Chronicling America: Historic American Newspapers, Library of Congress, http://chroniclingamerica.loc.gov/lccn/sn82015080/1886-08-27/ed-1/seq-2.
266. *Proceedings of the Thirteenth Annual Session of the Kansas Conference of Charities and Correction.* Lawrence, KS. (December 5 and 6, 1912). Topeka, KS: Kansas State Printing.
267. *Proceedings*, supra note 259.
268. *Phillipsburg Herald*, January 26, 1891.
269. Ibid.

INDEX

ABOUT THE AUTHOR

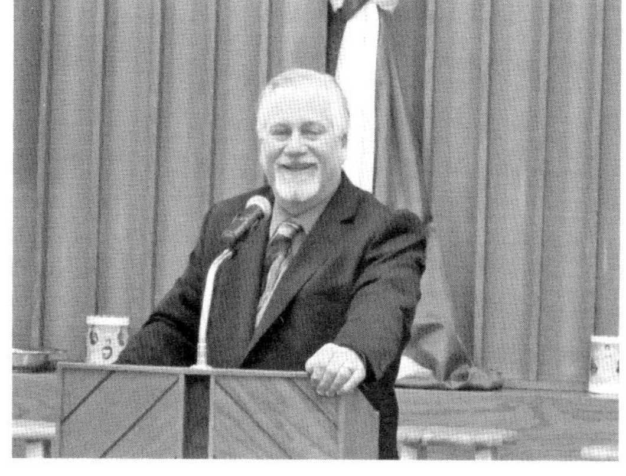

Gerald J. Bayens, PhD, is the associate dean of the School of Applied Studies and professor of criminal justice at Washburn University in Topeka, Kansas. He also provides direct services and technical assistance to criminal justice agencies, focusing on strategic planning and policy development.

Dr. Bayens served as a military policeman in the U.S. Marine Corps from 1974 through 1978. He worked in the criminal justice field for twenty-two years, in both law enforcement and corrections. His first job was as a narcotics special agent with the Kansas Bureau of Investigations. He then worked for the Shawnee County Sheriff's Office in Topeka, Kansas, as a deputy sheriff in narcotics investigations. Changing career paths from policing to corrections, Dr. Bayens worked for fifteen years at the county jail as a jailer, supervisor, manager and administrator. After accepting an offer to join the academic community at Washburn University, Dr. Bayens has worked as a teacher and mentor of students for the past twenty years.

ABOUT THE AUTHOR

Dr. Bayens is the author of numerous research articles, government reports and books. He is the recipient of the 1993 Washburn Alumni Fellows Award and 2014 A. Roy Meyers Excellence in Research Award.

Visit us at
www.historypress.net